The Power of Healing Prayer

Overcoming Emotional and
Psychological Blocks

THE POWER OF
HEALING PRAYER

Overcoming Emotional and Psychological Blocks

Richard McAlear, O.M.I.

Our Sunday Visitor Publishing Division
Our Sunday Visitor, Inc.
Huntington, Indiana 46750

Nihil Obstat:
Msgr. Michael Heintz, Ph.D.
Censor Librorum

Imprimatur:
✠ Kevin C. Rhoades
Bishop of Fort Wayne-South Bend
December 11, 2012

The *Nihil Obstat* and *Imprimatur* are declarations that a work is free from doctrinal or moral error. It is not implied that those who have granted the *Nihil Obstat* and *Imprimatur* agree with the contents, opinions, or statements expressed.

Stories included in this book are factual, but the names have been changed to protect the privacy of the individuals.

Unless otherwise noted, Scripture passages are the author's own translation.

ISBN: 978-1-61278-567-7 (Inventory No. T1265)
eISBN: 978-1-61278-310-9
LCCN: 2012953906

Cover design by Amanda Falk
Cover image: *Christ Healing the Blind*, English School (20th Century) / Private Collection / © Look and Learn / The Bridgeman Art Library

PRINTED IN THE UNITED STATES OF AMERICA

CONTENTS

INTRODUCTION

Why Pray for Healing?

In various places in the Gospels, the evangelists give us brief summaries of the life and ministry of Jesus, providing in one simple paragraph an overview of the larger story. Matthew tells us, for example:

> Jesus went throughout Galilee teaching in the synagogues, preaching the good news of the kingdom, and healing every kind of disease and illness among the people. News about Him spread all over Syria, and people brought to Jesus everyone who was ill with various diseases, those suffering with severe pain, the demon possessed, the epileptic, the paralytic, and He healed them all. Large crowds came from Galilee, from the Decapolis, Jerusalem, and Judea, and they even came from the regions across the Jordan, and they followed after Him.
>
> (Matthew 4:23–25)

We see here two dimensions of the ministry of Jesus. The first is called the ministry of the word. Jesus went about teaching and preaching everywhere — on the hillsides, on the lakeshore, in synagogues on both sides of the Jordan — always proclaiming the Kingdom of God. He was a typical rabbi of the time, both a preacher and a teacher. The teachings of the Lord form the basis of all theology to this day.

The second dimension of Jesus' ministry is what He did in the midst of His people. As Jesus went about, He healed all those who were sick and those who suffered from various torments. If one were to go through the four Gospels and underline the passages that speak of the healing ministry of Jesus, one might be surprised to find almost half of the text underlined.

This is why large crowds followed Jesus everywhere: People were desperate for healing, and Jesus healed. In Jesus they saw hope — hope that they could be released from their suffering and from their grief. Jesus never disappointed those who came to Him with that hope. Scripture tells us that *He healed them all.*

Jesus wanted His ministry to continue after the Resurrection and His return to the Father. He told the disciples at the Last Supper, "The work that I do, you will also do. And even greater works than these, you will do" (John 14:12).

The power of God's Spirit was poured out upon the disciples. It was the Spirit of Jesus, the Spirit of love. In that Spirit, and in the name of Jesus and with His authority, the community of the Church is to carry on — through the centuries and all over the world — the work Jesus did in Galilee for those three years. We know that Jesus' presence in the Church is authentic and living because of the work that the Church does in His name.

Yet if we look at the history of the Church, we find that the work of Christ has not always continued with the same great power that Jesus modeled. Christian compassion has given rise to many works of charity in the Church: caring for widows and orphans, running hospitals and schools, teaching and preaching, and caring for the sick and shut-ins. When it comes to healing, however, much has been relinquished to medical science.

There is nothing wrong with medical science, but there are at least two reasons why it is not enough and why we need a ministry of prayer for healing. The first is that some things simply cannot be touched by typical medical practice. We immediately think of such evils as cancer, Alzheimer's disease, AIDS, diabetes, and so forth, which are usually incurable. But on a more everyday note, there is still little we can do for a person with a fever beyond what Peter could do for his mother-in-law. So we need Jesus to come (see Luke 4:38–39).

A second reason why a ministry of prayer for the sick is necessary is that God *wants* to be directly involved with the alleviation of suffering. The very presence of Jesus on earth and the healing work He did show God directly intervening in people's lives to touch their afflictions.

Physical healing is the more obvious healing and is what readily comes to mind when we speak about healing. But there is also healing of the human spirit, of the mind, and of the soul. The Lord teaches His ministers of healing how to touch the hidden places of the heart with His love. Healing can even touch memories and the scars left by traumas of betrayal, abandonment, rejection, and violence.

The healing ministry is a concrete way of saying that God cares. He loves, and we are the people He loves.

1

THE HEALING MINISTRY OF JESUS

There are also many other things which Jesus did; were every one of them to be written, I suppose that the world itself could not contain the books that would be written.

John 21:25 (RSV)

The healing ministry of Jesus is important for many reasons, but especially because it tells us something about who Jesus is and why He came. Even many non-Christians are familiar with Jesus as a teacher who speaks of eternal truths and divine ethics. But Jesus is more than a teacher and more than a model of human life.

Church theology has stressed that the healing work of Jesus is a demonstration of His power. The works that He did prove that He is indeed the Son of God. They authenticate the words He spoke. His divinity demands that His message be taken seriously. When God speaks it is important to listen well.

Certainly there is a basis for this in Scripture. St. Paul tells us that "in Him dwells the fullness of divinity in bodily form" (Colossians 1:19). To hear Jesus is to hear the Father (see John 12:50).

The Gospel of John takes a slightly different approach. John speaks about the works of Jesus not so much as miracles and acts of power but rather as signs. "This was now the second sign that Jesus did when he had come from Judea to Galilee," the evangelist tells us after describing the healing of the official's son (John 4:54). In this sense the miracles and healings of Jesus go beyond the fact that He is the all-powerful Son of God to point to His identity as the Incarnation of a personal God who is love. Jesus is the embodiment of the compassion, the intense interest, and the fatherly concern that God has for His people. Healing is a sign of that love.

Jesus, as Love Incarnate, walks among a suffering humanity. In the midst of the suffering He encounters, Love can do no less than reach out to alleviate that suffering, to embrace, comfort, and console. The presence of Love in the midst of the world will always be a healing presence.

"God is love" (1 John 4:8), and Jesus is Emmanuel, which means "God is with us" (Matthew 1:23). Jesus is the love of God made manifest and real in our midst. Jesus comes to bring salvation. In Him the love of God touches the suffering of the world.

Jesus is the perfect fulfillment of all the hopes and possibilities of humanity. His very name speaks to us of His identity, His mission in its most essential sense. For the name *Jesus* means "God saves," "God is Savior," "God is Redeemer."

Savior of the World

The world God created, presented to us in the Book of Genesis, was a perfect world. The human race was created to be the crowning achievement of everything that God had made so wonderfully perfect. People were meant to be happy and fulfilled. They were to be at peace and at one with themselves, others, and the world that God made.

God created humans in this wondrous state and put them in a place called Paradise, or Eden. This place was the sign and symbol of all that was perfect, all that was good, and all that we think of as happiness. Genesis tells us that God would come and walk with man in the garden (see Genesis 3:8–9). This symbolizes the fact that man was created in the image and likeness of God. An intimacy and a bond of unity and love existed between them. That bond was the foundation of all that we consider to be Paradise. When man and God are linked in bonds of friendship, all is well and there is Eden — the perfect world.

Then we read of sin entering the world, causing a rupture in the relationship between God and humanity. God's world became spoiled; its beauty was marred. Sin increased, and sin abounded. The more man became alienated from God the Creator, the more people became alienated from one another and from the world in which they lived. Humans became alienated even within their own hearts, at peace neither with God nor with themselves.

The situation of a world without God, with man locked in his isolation, became a situation of increasing brokenness — broken lives, broken dreams, and broken hearts. The selfishness and sin of man wreaked havoc and gave birth to suffering. Man came into bondage to evil. Evil unchecked began to destroy, degrade, and dehumanize what God had made so good and so beautiful in His image and likeness.

God, however, is a God of compassion and love. He is committed to His creation and would not abandon His people, the work of His hands and the love of His heart. We read in the third chapter of John's Gospel that "God so loved the world that He sent His only Son, so that every soul who believes in Him would not perish but have life everlasting" (John 3:16). Our God is so good and loving that He could not leave His people in their brokenness, abandon them in their bondage to evil, or ignore their suffering. So He gave what was deepest within Him, His only begotten Son, in order to redeem the world, to mend its brokenness. His Son would put the world back together and restore it to the beauty that the Father had originally intended.

Jesus comes, as John tells us, not to condemn the world. He comes to redeem it from its sin and to restore its grace (see John 3:17). That indeed is the first healing work of Jesus, of which we must never lose sight. Jesus comes to restore humanity to the Father's love by the forgiveness of sin. He reestablishes the friendship with God that existed at the beginning. So the first and most important healing is not a physical one but a spiritual one.

Abundant Life

Jesus knows more than anyone else of a world that was created beautiful and whole. He is moved to anger at the bondage, the evil, and the brokenness that He finds in this world. And at every point Jesus restores people to wholeness. He rescues them out of their brokenness and pain. He heals.

Jesus comes not simply to save the world but to save the individual. Recall the healing of Peter's mother-in-law (see Luke 4:38–39). She was in bed with a fever when Jesus came to the house. Jesus went to her, took her by the hand, and rebuked the fever. Immediately she was made well.

Jesus calls every single person to Himself and back to the wholeness of life that God intends for all. When He finds people broken by disease, He heals their bodies. When He finds them in bondage to evil spirits, He casts out the evil spirits. When He finds them lost and alienated from God, He forgives their sin and reconciles them. He redeems people like Mary Magdalene from a life of degradation and Zacchaeus from isolation.

Jesus comes also to restore people's spirits and hearts. Recall, for example, the story of the widow whose only son had died. Jesus felt her grief, and He reached out and raised the dead boy to life. This was a healing of the broken heart of a lonely woman more than an act of power to prove His divinity (see Luke 7:12–15).

What God wants for His people is what the Jewish people call *chayyim*, which means "life." This is not just existence but life in its fullness, life with joy, life in abundance. Jesus proclaims that He has come to give this life in abundance (see John 10:10). God is not distant; He does not look down on the world from far away. Rather God is passionately involved in the world that He has made. He is deeply interested in His people and in their lives.

God compares His care to that of a shepherd for his sheep (Psalm 23; Isaiah 40:11; John 10:11–16). Even more than a father and mother care about their own child, and even more than a bridegroom loves his bride, so God is very much in love with His people.

> Can a woman forget her sucking child,
>> that she should have no compassion on the son of
>> her womb?
> Even these may forget,
>> yet I will not forget you.
> Behold, I have graven you on the palms of my hands.
>> (Isaiah 49:15–16, RSV; see Isaiah 62:3–5;
>> Hosea 11:1–4, 8–11)

Jesus restores a broken world. This is a perfect summary of His life's purpose. He heals because He loves. He needs to redeem and save what is lost and broken. It is what He is about and who He is.

Power in the Church

Jesus worked within the limits imposed by His human nature. He was just one person who ministered for some three years in a fairly confined geographical area, in the region of Galilee and around Jerusalem. So it was His plan to call others to share in His ministry to both expand and continue it.

In His own lifetime Jesus sent His disciples out to do the work of teaching and preaching and healing. We read that these disciples went forth, anointed people with oil, and cast out demons. They healed the sick and even raised the dead. And they came back rejoicing at all they had done and all they had witnessed (see Matthew 10:1–8; Mark 6:7–13; Luke 10:17–20). It was the same work Jesus was doing!

The Lord wanted His ministry to continue. He gave the Spirit of His love and power to His disciples for that very purpose. The Acts of the Apostles shows us that the early Church was, in fact, a continuation and an extension of the ministry of Jesus. The very first thing Peter and the apostles did was to preach as Jesus had preached: they proclaimed the great and wonderful deeds of God (see Acts 2:14–36). They prayed as Jesus had prayed.

The disciples also healed as Jesus had healed. Recall the story of the cripple at the temple gate who was begging for charity. We read that as Peter and John were about to go into the temple, the beggar asked them for alms. Peter said to the man, "I do not have silver or gold, but what I do have, I will give you." He took the man by the hand and said, "In the name of Jesus Christ, arise and walk." The beggar stood and followed Peter and John into the temple, praising God (see Acts 3:1–10).

St. Paul tells us that the ministry of Jesus has been shared among the believers in many ways through many ministries and gifts (see 1 Corinthians 12; 14). This work and ministry have continued in the Church through the centuries.

The healing ministry is very much a summary of what salvation truly means.

It is important to reach out in the name of Jesus to heal everything that would hinder the fullness of life or destroy beauty and human wholeness. So the healing ministry will always be an essential part of the Christian life and work.

Healing happens because God cares, because God is love, and because we are the people He loves. Jesus was passionate about healing. He would not let any obstacle or controversy deter Him from touching the sick and the hurting. Love can do no less.

A Ministry of Prayer, Faith, and Love

What does one mean when one prays and acts in the name of Jesus? It is much more than simply using the name of Jesus or repeating the name of Jesus. When Scripture speaks about going forth in the name of someone, it means that one speaks or acts as though that person were actually present.

For example, in those days a civil authority or ambassador would go forth in the name of the king. If such an emissary came in the name of the king, he was treated and received as the king himself would be. The ambassador would act as the king, and he could make treaties and promises in the name of the king. His word would have the same binding force as that of the king. It was as though the king himself were actually present in the person of his representative.

So those who went forth in the name of Jesus acted, spoke, and worked in the person of Jesus. Their prayer and word had the same power and binding force as the prayer and the word of Jesus Himself. This is what the Lord ordained. Even now He is present in those who preach, touch, and heal in His name.

No suffering person is overlooked or outside the watchful care of God. The Lord wants to affirm that truth, to show that He is present with compassion and mercy to His people. Jesus was present in Galilee to demonstrate that care and love of the Father. Now it is the minister, working in the name of Jesus, who shows the loving presence and providence of the Father. Through the minister, God is present to the suffering.

To minister the presence of Jesus, reaching out to heal in His name, is basically a ministry of prayer. No human being has the power to cure disease. Jesus does have that power, and we experience it through prayer.

The healing ministry is also a ministry of faith. This is not just doctrinal faith, which believes in all the dogmas and teachings of the Church, even though that is necessary. Nor is it a simply providential faith, an understanding that everything is going to work out in the end by God's grace. Rather, the healing ministry is a ministry demanding expectant faith, a faith that anticipates God's action in the here and now.

Finally, the healing ministry must be a ministry of love and compassion. It is a ministry caught up in the very love that God has for His people. The Gospels tell us that Jesus was moved by compassion to minister to the sick and the suffering (see Matthew 14:14; Luke 7:13). That is still the only valid motive for ministry.

Jesus did not offer a set of techniques on how to heal people. But He did teach about love. All those who live in the spirit of love can reach out and touch in the name of Jesus. It is a ministry of the heart.

Healing is prayer with one hand raised to the Father in faith and the other hand stretched out in love toward the sick. It is allowing oneself to be a minister of God's love, so that His love flows through one's heart and one's words. These are the essentials that will characterize the ministry of anyone who would act in Jesus' name: prayer, faith, and love.

And so we pray

> *Jesus, thank You for Your abundant love.*
> *Thank You for coming to us and manifesting the Father's love.*
> *We adore You, Savior of the world.*
> *We pray, lifting a hand to You in faith and a hand to our brothers and sisters in love.*

2

WHO CAN MINISTER HEALING?

The harvest is plentiful, but the laborers are
few; pray therefore the Lord of the harvest to
send out laborers into his harvest.

Matthew 9:37–38 (RSV)

The question naturally arises as to who should and who can
pray for healing in the name of Jesus. Should many, even
all Christians carry on the ministry, or is it only for a select
and privileged few?

St. Paul wrote in his letter to the Ephesians, "Praise be
to God whose power working within us can do infinitely
more than we could ever ask for or even imagine" (Ephesians 3:20). St. Paul had a strong sense of the power of God
that is at work within every Christian believer, not just an
exceptional one here and there. Every baptized Christian
is a temple of the Spirit of God, and Jesus lives within his
heart. The Spirit is not a passive, impersonal presence; He
works through the ministry of the baptized, to whom His
gifts have been confided.

Answering the Cry of the World

Though human situations vary, a common thread runs through them all: Sickness abounds. There is an abundance of not just physical disease but also mental and spiritual illness. People carry deep wounds and cry out for relief.

The world in which we find ourselves is different in many ways from the world Jesus faced in His time. We have made great advances in medical science, psychology, and health care. Yet those advances have not solved all the problems people face.

People are battered by an uncaring world. Many are bruised in spirit because of the pressures of society and life in general. How many people suffer from debilitating depression? How many abuse drugs and alcohol? How many reel from the effects of a nasty divorce? How many lonely souls live in the midst of crowds of people? Evil has a hold in many lives.

Some would ask, "If Christ were alive today, how would He respond to the situations in our world? If Christ were alive today, what would He do?"

The truth is that Christ *is* alive today — not walking the earth as He did two thousand years ago, but living in the midst of believers, by the power of the Spirit. And His response to today's situations is the same as when He moved about Galilee in the flesh. Christ came to heal and to save. Sin is not the definitive word, and the effects of sin are not the ultimate reality.

Jesus is still at work through His people. Christians of today should respond as Jesus Himself would and as Jesus in fact did. Thus a ministry of prayer to the sick and suffering, to the brokenhearted, to the crushed in spirit, and to those bruised by an uncaring society should be a normal activity of Church life.

The call from the hearts of people is urgent and persistent. It is a cry for relief and for hope. Every baptized Christian shares in the responsibility to minister to this broken world. The gifts of the Spirit are for everyone to use for everyone's benefit.

Who is capable of touching the sick with healing grace? That is the same as asking, "Who can sew, cook, or play tennis?" The answer is, of course, "Just about anyone." Some simply do it better than others.

Whether it is sewing, cooking, or playing tennis, some people feel their way along and can be more or less adequate. Others have an attraction to it and are more dedicated and involved. They do it better than others simply because they spend more time at it and concentrate harder. Then there are the professionals, those who center their lives on their talents and skills.

So it is with healing. Anyone in whom Jesus lives can lay hands on the sick and pray for healing. Indeed, all should lay hands on the sick and pray for them when God calls them to do so. But some will do it better and be more dedicated and more focused on it. These could be said to have a special calling to the healing ministry.

Gift and Ministry

A distinction needs to be made between the *gift* of healing and the *ministry* of healing. The gift is a power. Anyone in whom the Spirit of God lives has that power. The gift might not be very well developed; it might not be very strong. But it is a gift just the same.

Everyone can pray for healing, and everyone should when the occasion calls for it. A mother should lay hands upon her sick child; a husband can pray for his wife; anyone can pray for a friend who is sick. Each and every member of the Christian community has occasion to step out in faith, stretch out a hand to touch the hurting and the sick, and pray for healing with expectant faith.

A prayer group in New England had a very successful youth ministry. There were several groupings, based on age, from high school down to junior high and one for the even younger. There was dynamic leadership at the time and a great interest in the gifts of the Spirit. The youngsters learned to pray for healing, seemed to enjoy it, and were very willing to pray whenever the occasion called for it. They prayed for one another when there was sickness among them. They prayed for parents and for anyone who asked for prayer.

The style of prayer varied according to the ages of the children, but there was a purity of intention, a simplicity, and an openness to the movement of the Holy Spirit that astounded their elders. The young people would gather around and lay their hands on the one in need and simply ask God to bless and heal the person. It was very uncomplicated and straightforward. Most importantly, prayers were answered, and people were blessed.

This is proof that healing prayer does not require theological training or some special sophistication. Rather it requires simple faith and compassionate love. Even children can do it. Sometimes they can do it better because they are free of the fear and hesitation that hold adults back.

Within the body of Christ, however, there are not just various gifts but also different ministries. People who have a ministry usually spend their time and effort focused on that ministry, one to which they feel called. They develop their gift by using it in a consistent way and so gain experience and maturity in that ministry.

The healing ministry is for those who are dedicated to praying for healing. They take the time to minister at length to the sick and do so consistently rather than just occasionally. Usually the Church community recognizes these people as having the gift of healing in some special way. Not all of these are called to spend great amounts of time in ministry, but some are so called.

To have a ministry of healing is a special and holy work. It is for those whom the Lord chooses and whom He equips with the gifts needed to accomplish it. There is great mystery in God's call: He calls whom He chooses, for His own reasons and for His own purposes.

Qualities of a Healer

People can end up praying for healing for the wrong reasons, sometimes for self-serving reasons. The healing ministry can involve some degree of self-glorification, a lot of self-satisfaction, and not a little pride. There is no doubt that the healing ministry can be exciting: It usually involves being up front and very visible.

Anyone who prays for healing, on any level or to any degree, must act with serious intention and responsibility. Those who become involved in healing for the fame, for the excitement, and even for money may have success for a time, but such mixed motives do not produce long-lasting effects. An authentic minister strives to pray sincerely, with the pure motive of giving glory to God.

Four qualities distinguish a man or woman as an authentic minister of Christ. The first, very simply, is *love and compassion*.

Why should anyone stretch out his hand to pray for healing? What is the ultimate motive? It must be the same reason Jesus prayed and ministered healing: The minister has a sense of love and deep compassion for the suffering and the hurting.

Compassion leads to service. Authentic service is the forgetting of self to focus on another person in need. As Jesus said, "If I seek my own glory, it is nothing at all" (John 8:54).

Ultimately the power of God, the power of His Spirit, is the power of love, because God is love, and His Spirit is the Spirit of love. Jesus is the Incarnation of love. All that He did was a gift and demonstration of love. Love is the distinctive quality of all Christian ministry.

The second important quality in a minister of healing is *faith*. As previously described, this is not just a doctrinal faith that believes in teachings and dogmas, even though that is important. Neither is it so much a providential faith that feels that everything will work out well in the end because of the Father's watchful care. Rather, what is required is a faith of expectancy, a faith that reaches out with quiet confidence, with a serenity born of trust, and fully expects that God will hear prayer.

Love and faith in the heart bring power to healing prayer. Because of the quiet confidence in the presence of Jesus, where two or three gather and minister in His name (see Matthew 18:20), healing prayer can be very quiet and tranquil. It is not more effective if it is poetic or loud or if it quotes many Scriptures and is grammatically correct. Faith knows that God is present, that He hears, and that He works through His minister.

The third essential quality for a healing ministry is *humility*, which leads to a total reliance on God. Humility allows God to give the minister His healing power. Humility totally relies upon God's mercy, His love, and His fatherly care and not upon any special quality, talent, or ability of the minister. This is all God's work, and it is for His glory and His alone.

The minister needs to be aware that the will of God matters before all else. He or she must surrender to His will and rely on His grace. God has His own plan and His own purpose, and neither is always understood.

One time a woman named Luciana brought a friend to me for prayer. Luciana's friend was desperately sick. We prayed for healing, and for some unknown reason, Luciana was suddenly healed of a pain in her back that had debilitated her over the years, while the friend she brought seemingly received no obvious healing.

God does work in mysterious ways. It is very humbling to realize that no one can manipulate Him or control an outcome. The minister simply prays for the sick as the Lord instructs. Beyond that it is all up to Him.

A minister can be overwhelmed by the power of evil and feel totally inadequate. He or she might feel incapable of making a difference in someone's situation. That feeling of inadequacy can lead to a deep humility, as the only recourse is to rely solely upon the power of God.

Often I have been overwhelmed by the needs of people coming for prayer, by the magnitude of their brokenness. In such moments I need to step back and remember that it is God's work, not mine, and that these are His people. Surrendering to His mystery is an ongoing process, not a once-in-a-lifetime prayer. When the minister truly surrenders, God can work wonderful things through His imperfect, limited, but willing instrument.

The fourth quality required for the minister of healing is the *ability to allow God to act*. When we pray, we must allow God to have complete dominion over everything that takes place. God answers prayers as He sees fit.

Many people pray for healing and put very specific demands on God, expecting Him to do very specific things and wanting to limit Him to specific responses. Anything beyond the horizon of what they envision they find strictly unacceptable. These people are not asking God for an answer but telling God what to do and how and when to do it, then adding a list of what He is not allowed to do. Such people restrict God by their own narrowness and need.

God has His own mystery beyond human understanding. Sometimes He will answer a prayer in an unexpected way or with a response that challenges faith. For example, sometimes a person will die rather than experience healing. That is an answer, just not the one expected or desired.

Faith tells us that God responds with love in a way that He alone understands. This can be quite humbling, yet no one would ever grow in faith if it were all so very simple and humanly understandable. A god we can understand, one who acts according to a human program, is just too small. God is larger than we can imagine; He cannot be categorized or programmed.

Am I Worthy?

A man named Kyle once came for prayer. He had been deeply touched and spiritually moved to the point of tears. But as I began to pray, he immediately began to tell me why he was not worthy to receive anything from God. He ended the prayer quite abruptly. Kyle's sense of unworthiness overrode the working of the Spirit within him. He ultimately preferred to reject a blessing and a healing rather than have the humility to accept what God was doing in his heart.

So too, there are many people who do not pray for the healing of others because they feel unworthy. "God would never use me to minister to another." "God could never use me to heal someone." "I am not worthy."

The truth is that, indeed, we are all unworthy. If holiness were the necessary criterion for ministry, very few would be allowed to pray for healing. The fact is that grace is a free gift, and God uses whomever He wills. It is not necessary to be holy in order to be used by God. It is necessary only to be there — available, open and present, and reaching out in faith with compassionate love.

I know a woman named Anne who went into the hospital for an operation. The doctors had discovered a large mass on her kidney, and it had to be removed and biopsied at once. When Anne entered the hospital, the priest paid a visit, as he did with all new patients. Anne was not a fervent Catholic, but she did practice her faith after a fashion. She was frightened, and fear tends to activate whatever level of faith people have.

Anne asked the visiting priest if he would anoint her and pray for healing. The priest, being of a more modern bent, was very reluctant. He felt that Anne had come to the hospital for the operation, and that was God's answer for her. God could work through medicine and doctors and modern science but not through prayer. The latter was just so much superstition, he thought.

But he did pray for her and bless and anoint her, more to make her happy than out of any sense of faith. When it came time for the operation, there was nothing — no mass on which to operate. Anne had been healed, and she had known it when the priest blessed her.

The priest was shocked and even upset by the miracle done through his prayer. It led him to reevaluate his own attitudes and the preconditions operating in his faith. God has the freedom to channel His work, His love, and His healing power through ministry done in His name. He uses even the least faith-filled to do His work.

No one is worthy of God. But in one way or another, we are all called to work in the Spirit's power. Jesus can reach out and touch the suffering that the minister is humanly incapable of touching. He works through the hands and hearts available to Him.

St. Paul wrote to the Corinthians, "Examine yourself and see if you are really living in the faith" (2 Corinthians 13:5). He gave them one criterion for judging whether one truly lives in faith: "Do you really acknowledge that Jesus Christ is in you?" The minister of healing must acknowledge that Jesus Christ really dwells within and is the One who reaches out, touches, and heals.

And so we pray

> Lord God and Father,
> we once again surrender to You with open hearts and with
>   open hands.
> You call us to minister in Your name and to do the same
>   work that Jesus did in His ministry.
> How can anyone take up such a task? How can we presume
>   to continue His work?
> He was holy; we are not.
> He was divine and perfect; we are human and very sinful.
> He had divine power; we have human weakness.
>
> But You invite. You call.
> You challenge us to take up the task and continue His work.

*So not because of any human ability, not with any boasting
    or pride, we say yes.*
We will respond in humble faith to Your call and invitation.
*We rely not on ourselves, our training or abilities, our
    knowledge or holiness.*
We are willing to minister and work in Your name.
*Trembling, we rely completely on Your Spirit to lead, to
    guide, and to work through us.*
It is Your work, and it is Your people who are in need.

We look only to you and ask that You gently use us
*for the glory of Your name and for the benefit of Your
    people. Amen.*

3

How to Minister Healing

We read in the Gospels that Jesus ministered healing to the multitudes. The needs were great, seemingly overwhelming at times. Jesus wanted helpers. He empowered the apostles to minister in His name. He sent them out to preach and to heal, to cleanse lepers, and to cast out demons.

The disciples returned from their mission enthused, because the ministry was powerful, and their prayers were effective. They prayed for healing, and healing took place. They found that "even demons are subjected to us when we use Your name." Luke's Gospel tells us that Jesus too was filled with joy. He prayed, "I bless You, Father, Lord of heaven and earth, for what You have hidden from the learned and clever,

You have revealed to the simple and the childlike" (see Luke 10:1–24).

We should understand what happened with the disciples, because what they did, we are supposed to do. So how did they heal the sick and cast out demons?

We know what the disciples did, but we know precious little about how they did it. The Gospels tell us only that they used the name of Jesus and anointed with oil. The prayer that Jesus utters when they return, however, gives us insight into the nature of their ministry and ours.

The ministry that Jesus was calling for is not something that the learned and clever can uncover by research and study. Rather, the ministry is for the simple of spirit and the childlike. It comes from the heart rather than from the head.

Throughout the centuries many have attempted to understand the healing power of Jesus. People have looked for techniques, methods, or even an occult science or some secret knowledge that Jesus might have taught His disciples. One might hear a minister say, "Step out in faith, claim your healing, and you will be healed." Some people would teach that laying hands on the sick is the only way to pray for healing. Some ministers demand a definite and explicit response to their prayer. Others ask quiet acceptance of the prayer without any outward sign of that acceptance.

Relying on a technique probably arises from a combination of insecurity and the need to control. The truth is that there is no prayer formula. The healing power of Jesus, and hence that of His disciples, is not so much a technique as a working of the Spirit of Love. It is simply a deep compassion for people who suffer and a quiet confidence in the Father's love.

Search the Gospel stories to see how Jesus healed. What you will find is that there does not seem to be any one way of doing it. In more than half the cases, Jesus gave a command accompanied by a touch. In some instances it was a touch without a word, and at other times it was a word of command without a touch. Sometimes He touched the sick; sometimes they touched Him (see Matthew 8:3; 9:20, for example). Occasionally Jesus called upon a person's faith; other times He gave commands without asking for a faith response (Matthew 9:6, 27–30).

Jesus used physical things — some rather unorthodox. He put His finger in the ears of the deaf-mute and His saliva on the man's tongue (see Mark 7:33). He rubbed mud, made from His saliva, into the eyes of a man born blind (John 9:6).

Sometimes it seems as if Jesus did nothing, as in the story of the ten lepers who came to Him for healing. He simply told them, "Go and show yourself to the priest." As they went on their way, they discovered that they were healed. It seems to have happened quietly and in a hidden way (see Luke 17:12–15).

Whether it was a spoken word, a command, a touch, a gesture, or simply silence, healing happened, and people were deeply blessed. It is love that touched hearts, minds, and bodies. It is the love of Jesus that is important to imitate, not the technique.

We see in Scripture that Jesus met each situation differently, because each situation, and each person in each situation, was unique. Jesus was in communion with the Father, and He knew what was needed in each case. Jesus knew that each heart, each person, and each situation was special. Knowing the inner needs of each person would produce the appropriate approach to each.

Healing gifts include not only the gift of healing but also gifts of discernment, wisdom, healing touch, prophetic utterance, the word of knowledge, and especially the gifts of compassion and love. All these gifts and more are needed to effectively minister healing in the name of Jesus.

Let us examine some principles that should be kept in mind when praying for healing. These are not methods, nor are they techniques. They are simply qualities that characterize effective healing ministry. They define the way we should pray for healing.

Gentleness

The first principle is, quite simply, that of gentleness. The touch of Jesus is a tender and gentle touch, born of love and compassion. Gentleness does not intimidate and is neither harsh nor overbearing. Gentleness understands the fears and anxieties of the sick or suffering person and so reaches out with an assuring and loving touch. If more people who pray for healing remembered the basic principle of gentleness, the healing ministry could be much more effective.

Some ministers come on too strong. They minister with a sincere heart but are direct and loud. This is likely an indication of the ministers' insecurity. Instead of being reassuring and building confidence, they intimidate and frighten. In doing so, the gentle power of God's love and compassion is obscured, and healing is hindered more than facilitated.

I once knew a minister who had a great passion for healing. He read everything he could find on the subject, studied testimonials, and interviewed every minister of healing he knew. He prayed and meditated on the Scriptures. Finally he felt ready to minister healing.

Because of his intense studies, this minister felt a great deal of confidence. He was bold and directive in his ministry, telling people what they needed to do to be healed. The only problem was that for all the advice he gave and all the directives he issued, for all his preaching and teaching, some people got better and found healing, while others did not recover, and some even died.

So he became more insistent in his teachings and directives, bolder, and brasher. It was almost as though the more he lost confidence in his so-called knowledge, the more he insisted that the people were at fault for not following his teachings, not obeying his commands, and not accepting what he was giving them.

Finally this man collapsed in what could be called a breakdown. He lost faith in himself and in God. What really happened was that he lost faith in what he thought he knew and what he once understood as absolute.

The man recovered his faith in due time and became a much humbler and gentler minister of the Gospel. He came to realize that it was never about him but about faith and trust in Jesus. He learned that the greatness of God could not be reduced to pat answers and simple formulas. He surrendered to the will of God and the mystery of His ways, which made him less directive and overpowering.

The man actually became a more effective minister of healing, not because of what he knew but because he realized that he did not have all the answers. He simply ministered out of a compassionate heart, with trust that the Lord would always do the right thing for the one for whom he interceded. He became gentle and loving — much closer to the example of Jesus than the overpowering and overbearing style he had once used.

Touch

The second principle in praying for healing is the principle of touch, or as it is called in the Scriptures, "the laying on of hands." Jesus performed more than half of His healings with some kind of touch. At the end of Mark's Gospel, when Jesus sent out the apostles, He told them that those upon whom they laid their hands would recover (see Mark 16:18). We read in the Acts of the Apostles that when Ananias laid hands on Saul, "something like scales fell from his eyes and he regained his sight" (Acts 9:17–18, RSV). Touch is important in healing prayer because it conveys a human connection as well as the love that is the Spirit of God.

The laying on of hands is a gesture that is interwoven into the very life of the Church. In the sacraments it is the essential sign of imparting the Spirit. In the Sacrament of Baptism, we hear the words "Receive the Holy Spirit" as the minister lays hands on the baptized. In the new Rite of Reconciliation, the Church asks the priest to stretch out his hands over the penitent and pray at the moment of absolution. The sign of imparting the Spirit in Confirmation is once again the laying on of hands. A priest is ordained when the bishop imposes his hands on him.

In praying for healing too, whether in the Sacrament of the Sick or by lay persons, imposing hands is a meaningful sign that touches the very heart of the ministry. The act of touch is a fundamental sign, a sacramental sign almost, of imparting the Holy Spirit for healing. Touch is not magic, but it is a gesture of solidarity, friendship, and compassion. The Spirit of Love is the one Who brings healing to the sick, but the minister of healing does not stand at a distance. That would be intercession, not healing ministry.

Touch is reassuring, especially when a person is hurting. It is a natural way of bridging any distance between people. We put a hand or an arm on the shoulder of a loved one. We embrace; we hold; we pat an arm or a back; we shake hands with a friend. At a wake, touch is an essential part of the support people offer to the grieving. Words fail at such a time, so what remains are gestures such as a hug or the gentle holding of a hand.

Something in human nature needs touch. It expresses closeness and reassurance. So it is in the healing ministry. When done with gentleness, touch speaks a healing presence and imparts a healing power. It is a physical connection between people that is spiritual at the same time, because the Divine Spirit is present in the midst of the human love and compassionate prayer.

Where to touch the person is a question often asked. In general it is good to touch the area that hurts if possible and if it can be decently done. In the case of a headache, touch the head. For spinal pain, touch the back.

Touch, of course, should never be intrusive. In no way should it make the person feel uncomfortable. One must be respectful and decent and not violate boundaries. In sensitive cases, just holding hands suffices to make the necessary human connection. Jesus touched and healed. We try to follow His lead.

Positive Prayer

The third principle applies to the actual prayer for healing. Like all prayer, it should focus on the love of God and the fatherly care of God through Jesus. The prayer can be addressed to Jesus or to the Father through Jesus. It can likewise be addressed simply to God.

The prayer will depend on what is comfortable according to the spirituality of the one who prays. Essentially it should be prayer that is focused on the Lord and His love and that expresses faith. The rest follows personal style and preference. Sometimes prayer is silent rather than verbal. It may be a pleading from the heart, with "groans and sighs that cannot be put into words," as St. Paul says (Romans 8:26).

It is all too easy to focus on illness and its effects — the pain and suffering, the danger to life, and the fear of death. This type of prayer can be very negative. It tends to magnify the evil of the illness.

On the contrary, the minister must look beyond the illness and raise the person's mind and heart to God with hope and confidence. Healing prayer focuses on the Father and His love. It emphasizes Jesus, His lordship, His power, and His will to heal. Healing prayer celebrates and recalls the truth that God is present, that He loves and cares for each and every one of His children, that He desires only life and peace for all, and that He forgives the sinner.

Authentic prayer gladdens the heart and strengthens faith by glorifying the Lord, who is over all things and who loves all. St. Paul tells us to pray always with thanksgiving and with praise: "Rejoice always, pray constantly, give thanks in all circumstances; for this is the will of God in Christ Jesus for you" (1 Thessalonians 5:16–18, RSV).

An essential quality to the prayer for healing is simplicity. Prayer should come from the heart. There is no need to be caught up in trying to compose eloquent prayers that are theologically accurate and grammatically correct. Eloquence does not move God; love does; faith does. One should simply be open to the leading of the Spirit and pray from the heart with quiet confidence and deep trust.

Let's look at two examples from Scripture. Lazarus was sick, and his friends sent a message to the Lord: "Lord, the one You love is sick" (John 11:3). This is a very simple, direct prayer, not long or involved. It is born of love and appeals to the love in the heart of Jesus.

The other prayer is that of the man who asked Jesus to come and heal his son: "I beg you to look upon my son, for he is my only child" (Luke 9:38, RSV). It is a similar prayer, though it is focused not on God's love for the person but on the man's love and concern for his boy. This prayer is spoken with confidence that the Lord, in His compassion, cares just as much for the sick boy as his father does.

Both these prayers result in healing. They give us models of simple prayers that stand on faith and love as a foundation. Anyone can use these as his or her own prayers for healing: "The one I love is sick. The one You love is sick. Come and heal."

Teamwork

Another principle to keep in mind when praying for healing is teamwork. God works in His Church, and He uses individuals for His work. But no individual is isolated and independent of a community. A person may have great gifts at work, but no one has all the gifts. On some level we always need other people and other gifts to complete the ministry. We need to rely on one another, each supplying a part of the whole so that the whole body is built up in strength, as St. Paul notes (see Ephesians 4:15–16).

A woman I'll call Clarice felt that she had the gift of healing. She advertised in a way, spreading the word that she was available to pray with the sick and the hurting. It was a private ministry in her home, unconnected to any community, church, priesthood, or leadership. She simply prayed by herself.

Problems eventually arose that Clarice could not deal with. One person collapsed while being prayed over and almost died. To another, Clarice gave advice that was ruin-ous and destructive.

Clarice neglected her duties in the house. Her children felt alienated because of all the people who were constantly in their home. Eventually her husband divorced her, one daughter ran away from home, and another daughter be-came pregnant out of wedlock. In the end the good woman herself suffered a nervous collapse and was hospitalized.

The lesson is well learned that no one should minister alone. We need one another.

It is important to seek unity in prayer and in ministry; otherwise there is no teamwork, only competition among people with different gifts. The team must pray with one heart and one voice before the Lord. Jesus says, "Wherever there are two or three gathered in the name of the Lord, agreeing upon anything, it will be done" (see Matthew 18:19–20).

Some people pray together but contradict one anoth-er. One might pray for a miracle and a healing, while an-other prays for a quiet, happy death. The question of what to pray for is not always easy to answer. That is why leader-ship and communication are necessary within the team. The team should reaffirm the prayers of one another. The prayers should interlock, and the *Amen* said at the end of the prayer time should be an affirmation that the ministers stand in solidarity before the throne of God, with united hearts and with one spirit.

Imagination

Still another principle is the use of the imagination. Some-times it helps while praying to form pictures and visualize what is happening. Many saints encouraged this use of imag-ination in prayer.

When praying for the sick, it is helpful to picture Jesus beside the sick person. Imagine Jesus reaching out His hand and touching the person's affliction or holding the person in a loving embrace. Allow Jesus to move and to act. Imagine what He would do and say. This is not an act of fantasy, because Jesus is indeed present and is doing something. Ask the Holy Spirit to show you what that is.

Another use of the imagination is to picture the healing light of God or the flow of God's love moving into the sick person — touching, bathing the afflicted area, and bringing healing. At some point in the prayer, the minister should picture the person healed and well, going about daily activities. This presents a goal for the prayer and builds up faith.

I have been present when a person praying for healing had the gift of vividly describing the action of the Spirit — the flowing light, the person experiencing healing, the disease vanishing. As others, and especially the sick person, heard the prayer, a new sense of faith, expectancy, and hope was engendered in everyone present. We all could visualize the action of the Spirit, and our unity in faith and in prayer allowed us all to focus on the same outcome.

Open and Grateful Hearts

A final principle is to be open to deeper and ever greater dimensions of healing prayer. There is always the need for deeper peace, for greater faith, as well as for joy, love, and forgiveness. After praying for physical healing, there should also be prayer for emotional and spiritual needs, allowing the Lord to minister in these areas. Chapter 5 deals more extensively with inner healing.

Healing prayers should always conclude with a prayer of deep thanksgiving and gratitude. There is a confident assurance that the Lord has heard the prayer. The Lord will answer with wisdom and in His own time. But He will answer.

And so we pray

Lord Jesus, we bring before You in our prayer one whom we love and You love. He is in need of Your healing touch. Let Your Spirit be at work here where He is most needed.

We are limited and weak and, in fact, helpless before this sickness. Your power alone can heal and touch and restore the one we love. We stretch out our hands in Your name, with love and hope. Let Your Spirit work in great power to heal and restore.

We thank You for Your love, for Your compassion, and for Your presence. We surrender this situation to Your care and to Your tender compassion. Please turn our anxiety to joy, our hope to rejoicing, our prayer of petition to a prayer of praise and thanksgiving. Right now we thank You for hearing this prayer, and we thank You for answering. Amen.

4

THE CHURCH'S MINISTRY

Now you are the body of Christ and
individually members of it. And God has
appointed in the Church first apostles,
second prophets, third teachers, then
workers of miracles, then healers, helpers,
administrators, speakers in various kinds of
tongues.

1 Corinthians 12:27–28

The question sometimes arises, why do we need a healing
ministry in the Church? Why should a frail and sinful human
being pray with another human being for healing? Could not
the sick person simply pray? Novena prayers and saints' intercession, Mass and Communion, and private prayers can
be effective and powerful. What then does another person
praying and imposing hands add to one's personal devotions?

The same line of reasoning occurs when the topic is
confession, the Sacrament of Reconciliation. People ask why
we cannot confess directly to God. Why go to another human person, a sinner like everyone else, to confess one's sin
and receive absolution?

Ultimately the question is why there should be any ministry in the Church and how the mediation of one person becomes a privileged channel of love and grace. This is really a question about the very nature of the Church as the body of Christ. For an answer we look to the Scriptures and to Jesus.

First, Jesus Himself ministered healing — touching the sick personally, one at a time. His power went out to heal them. This is simply what Jesus did on earth.

Secondly, Jesus commissioned the apostles and His disciples to do the same. His example and His command form the basis of all healing ministry. Praying for healing is not anyone else's idea or invention. It is a response of obedience to the will of Jesus as much as it is a response to the needs of the sick.

Finally, ministry is called for by the very nature of what the Church is — a community of faith that lives in love and serves the needs of all. This love and service explicitly continue the work of Jesus and respond to His direct command:

> Jesus, having loved His own in the world, now wished to show them the full extent of His love.... He poured water into a basin and began to wash His disciples' feet, drying them with the towel that was wrapped around Him....
>
> When He finished washing their feet, He returned to His place and said to them, "You understand what I have done for you. You call me teacher and Lord and rightly so, for that is what I am. Now I, your Lord and teacher, have washed your feet. You also should wash one another's feet. I have set an example for you. You should do as I have done for you."
>
> (John 13:1, 5, 12–15)

Here we have a beautiful lesson of what it means to minister. No task is too lowly or too demeaning for the Lord. He is the Savior, and He will wash His disciples clean of their sins and heal them of their sickness. He will unburden them of their guilt and make them clean.

Jesus explains that His actions are meant to be an example for the disciples. What He did must become a model for their behavior, their relationships, and their work. They need to understand that serving others is at the very heart of Jesus' love. His command to share His love is essential to the life of the Christian community. They now need to go out and do as He did — serve and minister to one another in His name.

Serving One Another

The word *minister* comes from a Latin word that means "to serve." When Jesus speaks of ministering, He speaks of serving in love and meeting the needs of others. This is a core idea for the Church as community. For every need there will be a ministry to meet that need. If there is sickness, there will be a ministry of healing. If there is sorrow, there will be a ministry of consolation. If there is hunger, there will be a ministry to feed the hungry. These are works that love inspires.

On the material level the Church meets the needs of the poor, the homeless, the dispossessed, and the hungry. She also serves the spiritual needs of people, such as the needs for forgiveness, for instruction, and for spiritual guidance. Then there are all the hurting and wounded souls that cry out to be healed. The ministry of prayer uses the spiritual gifts, or charisms, to meet these needs.

No one asks why people do not meet their own physical and material needs directly, without the help of another person. We instinctively know that, in the normal course of events, ministry must be person-to-person. Doctors must use their art to heal. There are ministries to young and old, help for the weak and the poor among us. Yet people do wonder why spiritual things do not come directly from God but must be mediated through the community within human relationships.

When we ask if God answers when a person prays directly to Him, the answer is yes. He always has, and He always will. However, another dimension of prayer involves relationships and the Church community as it communicates God's love. This is the will and the plan of God as it unfolds in Scripture.

What does Jesus want His Church to do? What has He given over to His community as both a commission and an inheritance?

On the day of Pentecost, the Holy Spirit was poured out on the Church, and along with the Spirit came a multitude of gifts and ministries. These are the gifts and ministries that stand at the heart of the life of the Church. They are found within the institutional structures as well as in freely given charisms graciously inspired by the working of the Holy Spirit.

The sacraments, the seven pillars of the Church, stand as the very constitutive elements of the Church. One of those sacraments is the Sacrament of Healing, that is, the Anointing of the Sick. The essential tradition of the Church, formalized and encoded in its practice, has been to pray one-on-one for the sick and to ask God for healing. The priest administers this sacrament.

Another dimension of prayer for healing is ministry to one another within the community. This is not a sacrament but a prayerful practice among brothers and sisters in Christ — lay, ordained, and religious. A sick man or woman should be able to turn to someone in the Church community for prayer and a healing touch. This should be the normal life of the Church community: people praying and ministering to one another in faith and in love.

Why are there so many sick people in the world? Why is there suffering? Is it because God does not care or that He is not present?

God has given the power to heal, the authority to heal, as well as the commission to heal to the Church. He has given us a mandate to go out and lay hands upon the sick that they might be cured. The problem is not that we do not know how or that we do not have the capacity, the gift, or the authority. What is lacking seems to be the will to do what God has asked and the faith to take up the call. With deep patience God waits for us to take what He has given us and do what He has asked us to do: minister to the sick with prayerful faith and with a healing touch.

God calls us at this time in history to highlight the ministry of healing prayer. One reason for this is that healing prayer is part of a deep current of God's Spirit in the Church today, teaching the Church how to be Church. Each believer is part of the body of Christ and therefore part of one another. There are no isolated Christians.

Recognize the Body of Christ

I clearly remember a woman I'll call Jean who was part of the charismatic renewal for several years, experiencing in that movement a deep sense of God's love and His presence in her life. At some point Jean left the prayer community in which she had been involved, saying that she had outgrown the group and no longer needed a community. She still practiced the faith, with the hope of moving into a more personal, individual relationship with God.

Then Jean contracted cancer. She prayed to God for healing. She made novenas, and she went to Mass. She was not healed, and the cancer grew.

Finally the Lord spoke to her, and Jean felt called back to her prayer group. She made something of a public admission that she had felt that she had God and that was enough. But she had come to realize her real need for the community.

A priest anointed Jean in the Sacrament of the Sick, and the community gathered around her, imposed hands, and prayed for healing. The cancer was instantaneously healed. Years later it has not returned.

Jean came to recognize the body of Christ and her place in the body. Even though it is essential to have a personal relationship with the Lord, we need to have a relationship with the community of the Lord as well.

St. Paul's first letter to the Corinthians says of the Eucharist: "Do you receive in an unworthy way? Do you recognize the body?... If you do not recognize the body, you eat and drink your own condemnation. No wonder there is sickness among you: you don't recognize the body" (1 Corinthians 11:27, 30). We can apply Paul's words to the community of the Church. Do you recognize the Church community as the body of Christ? If you do not, there will be sickness among you.

The truth is that Jesus mediates His love through our brothers and sisters. We need the humility to go to a brother or sister in our Church community and seek prayer, even though the one who prays is as weak and as prone to sickness as we are. Communities of people are frail, but community is where Jesus wants to be. That is where Jesus has chosen to make His home. "My power is made perfect in weakness" (2 Corinthians 12:9).

In the healing ministry the Lord calls us to a deeper sense of His presence and His work within one another. This sense is essential to all spiritual growth. The healing ministry leads to deeper insight into the heart of the Church's identity.

The minister of healing, a very human and weak sinner like everyone else, is one who reaches out in the name of the Lord and is confident in the presence of a loving Father and a loving Savior. The minister who prays for healing does not rely on personal inner power or holiness but rather is an instrument who prays in faith. God is pleased to confirm that faith, and so healing takes place.

God has not forgotten His people. He is not far away. He is in our midst and very much at work through the ministers who act in His name.

And so we pray

Jesus, I stand in awe at the mystery of Your ways. You call me, and all of us, to minister in Your name, to reach out with Your touch, to love with Your heart. You want me to be Your voice, Your heart, and Your hands and feet. You call each of Your children to responsibility and maturity as members of Your body, the Church.

I want to recognize in myself the power of Your presence: not my holiness or abilities or talents but Your presence at work within me and through me. This is very humbling, because I know my sin and my weakness. Yet I must trust that You work through even the weakest and most sinful by Your Spirit's power.

I recognize that You are also at work in the other members of the Church. As sinful as I am, yet called and used by You for the work of grace, I can turn to others in the Church for blessing, support, and prayer. Do not let me ever be too proud to receive ministry from other sinners like myself. You work through them, and You work through me. It is all a wonderful mystery of love and grace.

Thank You for Your heart poured out in love for us all. I want to pour myself out for others as You did for me. Thank You.

5

INNER HEALING

The spirit of the Lord has been given to me.
God has anointed me,
sending me forth to bring good news to the
    poor,
to bind up hearts that are broken,
to proclaim liberty to captives
and freedom to those who are imprisoned.

Isaiah 61:1–2

Jesus used this Scripture passage to proclaim His identity and His ministry when He returned to His hometown of Nazareth and preached for the first time (see Luke 4:16–21). For Jesus, this passage expresses what He was about, what He was to do, and why He was to do it. Importantly, the passage speaks specifically not about healing physical diseases but about healing broken hearts and freeing captives.

Certainly there is a need for healing of all manner of physical ailments, but this is only one dimension of a much bigger picture. Jesus is ultimately interested in human wholeness. The desire of His heart is to restore people to the fullness of life that God His Father originally intended everyone to have. Beyond physical healing there is *inner healing*, which includes healing a broken heart, healing a crushed and bruised spirit, as well as healing a wounded soul.

People in the world today suffer from painful memories and from sorrowful and grieving spirits. Many are prisoners of their own fears and anxieties. People carry wounds in the depths of their hearts, unseen but still very real. Many are crushed under burdens of guilt and feelings of worthlessness. Many seethe with resentment, spite, and even hatred. These are all prison cells that hold people captive.

Jesus' love embraces people at every level of their experience. He wants to touch all the painful feelings and hurting memories that wound and debilitate. Jesus wants to touch the human spirit with healing love, with forgiveness, and with a gentle power that sets people free from all that would bind and hold them captive.

Real Pain

There are two dimensions to the necessity of prayer for inner healing. One is the role of inner pain in physical sickness. The other is the inner pain and anguish itself.

First of all, it is important to realize that many of the physical sufferings afflicting the body may be caused by something deeply rooted within the person's psyche. Scientific studies assert that up to 80 percent of all illness is psychosomatic. Psychosomatic illness is very real; it is not imagined. There is real pain and real disease, which can show up in blood work and x-rays. But the roots of the problem run deep; the physical problem is connected to something within the heart and soul of the person.

For example, anxiety, nervous tension, and stress can either cause or aggravate an ulcer. In such a case, healing prayer needs to go deeper than the physical realm. We must pray too for the unhealed part of the spirit that causes the anxiety and fear that contribute to the ulcer. If we do not attend to the whole complex of issues, the healing will be incomplete at best.

When I first began praying for healing, now many years ago, my prayer community would sponsor healing services, and everyone would be involved in some way in the prayer. There was one young man, William, who always helped with the services but suffered himself from a debilitating ulcer. There were hosts of foods he could not eat, and he was always taking medication for the condition. The problem limited what William could do and the places he could go.

It is a well-known fact that people who pray for others are the last to ask for prayer for themselves. One night after the healing service was over, however, William was in a great deal of distress because his ulcer was "acting up," as he put it. Someone suggested we pray over him. So the team gathered around and prayed for William, and he was instantaneously healed. He felt it in his body and knew it in his heart.

To test the healing William ate some pizza, and he had no adverse effects. He drank cola and ate some other foods that were always off limits to him. Again, there were no adverse effects. He was indeed healed. It was a cause for joy to him and to all his friends in the community.

All went well for about a month, and then William started to experience symptoms again. Indeed, after two months the ulcer was back. Although dismayed, the team prayed over William again, and he was healed once again of the ulcer. But in a few months the ulcer reappeared. This was troubling and led to a great deal of thought and prayer.

What became apparent was that William was highstrung and always stressed out. Sometimes it was because of his job, sometimes family concerns, and sometimes his relationships. William was not losing his healing, but he was getting ulcers anew from the stress and tension in his life. He had to complete the healing by learning to deal with stress.

The Lord was teaching us all a lesson, and that is that underlying causes for sickness need to be taken into account and dealt with. Besides praying for healing, it is important and necessary to minister to the person. That means taking time to listen to the person, offer counsel, and pray for the wounds of the heart. Inner-healing prayer addresses the brokenness, the painful memories, and the grief within. It is ministry to the inner self — the soul, the spirit, and the heart.

Inner-healing prayer can effect physical healing, because some illnesses are caused by inner conflict, hatred, repressed anger, and other issues. If the inner pain and turmoil can be resolved through prayer, the physical ailment is oftentimes resolved. In the case of William, people in the prayer group prayed with him, spoke with him, listened to him, and advised him on how to deal with certain problems in his life. These were not highly trained professional people but simply friends who took the time to listen and pray and support William on his life journey. In time, with support, prayer, and a lot of patient love, William became more peaceful and centered on the Lord, and he was completely healed of the ulcers.

One of the saddest things to see in the healing ministry is people coming for prayer but not being healed because deeper issues have not been addressed. Physical illness intertwines with psychological wounds and spiritual needs. For example, an extremely lonely person might need to be sick in order to gain sympathy, attention, and some outward semblance of love. A prayer for that person's healing will generally not be effective until the loneliness of the heart is touched and the emptiness of the soul is filled.

I remember the case of a fairly young woman who came to our house of prayer because she was in desperate need of healing. Christina was estranged from her family, and she had no real friends or social life because she was always sick from unspecified illnesses. The list of symptoms was long, including headache, fever, and upset stomach, and the doctors could never find a cause or cure.

Christina showed up unannounced at the house of prayer one day to ask for prayer. It happened to be a day when everyone who was available had come to do spring cleaning. We planned to go through the whole facility dusting, mopping, polishing, and so on. Christina was told that everyone was busy, but she could stay and help if she so chose.

Well, she did stay and help for hours with various tasks. As the people worked, there was laughter and friendly banter. She was caught up in the atmosphere and felt very much at home, accepted, and needed. When the day ended, Christina realized that she had done things, such as working with cleaning fluids and dust, that normally would have set off her immune system and caused violent allergic reactions. The conversation and relationships seemed to have taken her attention and obscured the other problems.

Christina became a regular at all the events and services of the center, and she actually became a valuable member of the team. She found acceptance, friends, purpose, love, a whole new life. The majority of her physical problems resolved themselves.

Life and people are too complex for simple solutions, of course, but there are many cases where healing involves the larger involvement of people in community — people who meet the needs of wounded hearts of broken people. Healing prayer must always be open to healing ministry, which gives a larger and broader context for the prayer.

A Healing Process

The second dimension of inner healing is also important. Sometimes the hurts of the heart are not the cause of physical problems or distress, but they are debilitating in themselves. Inner pain keeps many people from experiencing the joy of life and human wholeness. They are not free to be all that God created them to be. Such people quite simply need to be healed.

There is a mystery of brokenness in this world so wounded by sin — broken hearts, broken lives, broken relationships, broken marriages, and broken dreams. All this brokenness causes hurt, loneliness, pain, sorrow, and grief. Perhaps this is the human condition, but the truth is that Jesus came that we might have life and have it in its fullness (see John 10:10). He desires that there be ministry to the deep and hidden places within the person. This is the prayer for inner healing.

Jesus Christ is the same yesterday as He is today (see Hebrews 13:8). He transcends time, so He can move into a person's past in order to touch hurtful memories and traumatic incidents. It is His desire to set people free from the wounds and scars of the past.

Past and present tend to merge in the human person, within the heart. Experiences good and bad affect the way one thinks and responds to life in the present. Painful memories cannot simply be repressed and forgotten; if they are not healed, they lie buried in the subconscious, from which they can negatively affect one's behavior and thinking as well as one's emotional state.

"Inner healing" refers to the healing of the traumatic memories of life and their effects, such as the pain of abandonment, loneliness, anxiety, and fear. Inner healing means going back and filling the moments in life that lacked love and understanding. Inner healing fills in the gaps between the love that was needed and the love that was received.

A painful memory or hurtful experience is considered healed when it no longer has a negative effect on the person. The painful experience is neutralized, so to speak. The person realizes that it has lost its poison and no longer causes pain and sorrow. Then the person moves to a deeper healing, from which the experience can be seen in a positive light. The person can actually give thanks to God for it.

It is always possible to draw something positive from a painful experience, knowing that "all things work out for the good for those who love God" (Romans 8:28). A hurtful experience can become a source of deeper compassion for others who hurt. Someone who grieves can understand another person who grieves. It is possible to give thanks for such an experience, whether it was thought of as positive or negative at the time it happened.

Imagination

In praying for inner healing, a most important tool is the use of vivid imagination. Aristotle said that the imagination is the door to the inner soul. St. Thomas Aquinas taught that the imagination is the one faculty of the mind that has a two-fold aspect: It partakes of the inner life of the spirit and so draws from deep within the soul; at the same time it resides in the physical realm, the mind. Imagination is the convergence of the spiritual and material worlds.

Imagination allows a person to picture things that have deep roots within the inner self. Think of how dreams can be very vivid in imagery and feelings. At the same time, dreams flow from an inner source, deep within the soul or the subconscious. Dreams are the active imagination at work. The inner soul, the depth of the human spirit, uses real and tangible images to express itself.

Those who pray for inner healing have learned well the truth of these statements. A person can relive a memory, going back to a time that was hurtful, a moment of darkness and pain. In one way the memory cannot be changed without doing violence to reality. What happened has happened; what was, was. Yet it is possible to reimagine the experience in a new way.

Jesus can be brought into the scene using the imagination. It is the same memory, the same experience, but the soul embraces the larger reality and deeper truth that Jesus was indeed there. His presence was not realized at the time because the hurt was the primary experience.

Now, in prayerful imagination, the light of Christ can be brought into a moment of darkness. Incarnate love can be brought into a moment that desperately needed love. Forgiveness can be brought to a deep hurt that still lies buried in the heart. As the secure presence of Jesus is brought into a time of anxiety and fear, the effects of that anxiety and fear are removed.

Using creative imagination is not the same as fantasy. It is not pretending that Jesus was there. The fact is that Jesus *is* present at every moment and in every experience of life, the happy and joyful moments as well as the painful ones. Whatever life has brought — with whatever pain, sorrow, or sense of abandonment — the truth is that Jesus was there to minister His love and His forgiveness. Perhaps faith was lacking at the time, or the heart was closed and unresponsive, or more likely, the hurt was the more overwhelming experience. The prayer for inner healing brings to conscious awareness the love that was present but not realized or experienced.

In inner healing prayer the imagination allows the person to vividly picture what actually and truly was: Jesus present but not experienced. In prayer the memory is recalled but in its fullness. Where there was a lack of love in the past, the love and the understanding of Jesus now can fill that gap. Where there was a sense of abandonment and loneliness, the presence of Jesus now can bring security. Where there was anxiety and fear, the love of Jesus can now bring peace. Jesus frees the wounded soul from all the effects caused by hurt, betrayal, loss, rejection, and all the empty pursuits of the past. Jesus has been with us from the moment of our conception through every experience of our lives.

> Cry and the Lord will answer.
> Call out and He will say, "I am here."
>
> … Your light will rise in the darkness,
> your shadows will become like noon.
> The Lord will guide you.
> He will give you relief in desert places.
> He will give strength to your bones….
> What was ruined will be rebuilt;
> He will rebuild on the old foundation
> and what was once ruined will be restored.
>
> (Isaiah 58:9, 10–11, 12)

And so we pray

Father, I come to You holding many hurts and wounded by many painful moments in the past. These experiences still influence me today and hold me bound. I desire to taste a new freedom, new life, and new hope.

You have always been with me, at every moment and in every experience. You were never absent, never far from me. But there were moments when I experienced anxiety more than peace, turmoil more than loving acceptance, fear more than tranquility. The thoughts and heartaches of life overwhelmed me and blocked Your love and presence from my consciousness.

Come and enter into the dreadful moments of my past when I needed You most and was most unaware of You.

Try to remember a time and place that was painful and caused hurt. Picture the place and the people involved. Remember how you felt — all the emotions that were running rampant within you. Then imagine Jesus with you at that moment. Picture Him standing there, looking with love and compassion and understanding. He has total acceptance of you and total love for you.

Jesus, come to me and hold me in Your arms, in Your secure embrace. Hold me and let me feel safe with You. I have no fear, no condemnation, no judgment, no blame — just Your love and understanding. You know what is happening to me and around me, and You are here, telling me not to be afraid.

Jesus, I trust You in this moment and entrust everything to Your heart. Thank You for being here and loving me, protecting me and accepting me.

6

THE DECISION TO BE HEALED

There is in Jerusalem, near the sheep gate, a pool which in Aramaic is called Bethesda, surrounded by five porticoes. A great number of disabled people were accustomed to lie there — the blind, the lame, the paralyzed — all waiting for the stirring of the waters, for when an angel of the Lord stirred the waters, the first one into the pool was healed. One man was there who had been an invalid for thirty-eight years. When Jesus saw him lying there, and learned that he had been in this condition for a long time, He asked him, "Do you want to get well?" The invalid replied, "Sir, I have no one to help me into the pool when the water is stirred. While I am trying to get in someone else goes down ahead of me." Jesus said, "Get up. Pick up your mat and walk." The man was cured. He picked up his mat, and he walked.

John 5:2–9

Several unusual elements make this story stand out in contrast to other healing narratives in the Gospels. First, this is the only healing story in the Gospels where Jesus initiates the encounter. The man does not seek out Jesus and does not ask to be healed; rather Jesus approaches him and asks him a question.

And the question He asks is an interesting one: "Do you want to get well?" We might assume that a man who has spent thirty-eight years as a cripple and who is waiting to get into the healing waters would want to be cured. Surely Jesus knew the circumstances of this man's life. He could read the man's heart, and He understood the man's thoughts and attitude. Yet Jesus felt the need to ask the man if he really wanted to be well. So there must be a deeper significance to the question.

Why would Christ ask that question? We have a possible hint in the answer that the man gave: "I have no one to help me. Someone always gets in before me."

"I have no one." It is the sad admission of a man who feels alone, abandoned, and isolated. It seems that everyone in his life has deserted him.

"Someone always gets there before me" is another sad statement, one tinged with self-pity. It seems that the man was as paralyzed emotionally as he was physically. That is why Jesus asked him if he wanted to be well. The man needed to decide for himself whether to break out of his isolation and loneliness and begin to walk again.

In any healing process, whether medically, in counseling, or in a ministry of prayer, a time of decision is necessary. The suffering person must decide to reject infirmity and choose health. In cases where such a decision is lacking, sickness can become an identity and in time a trap.

Discerning the Choice

Two points can be made about this decision to be healed. One is that the decision is not an emotional one, based on a feeling. It is an act of the will, a choice: "I want to be well." It is a purposeful choosing to move into a mentality of wholeness. The emotions will follow.

The second point is that a person should not be challenged to make that decision to be well unless there is true discernment that such a decision needs to be made. There are most definitely people for whom sickness has become a comfortable identity, but that is not everyone. Acting rashly runs the risk of putting guilt on people who do not deserve it.

The general principle is that God does want us well. He wants His people whole. He wants His children to be healthy, living full, rich lives. However, general principles have exceptions. So before challenging a person and demanding a decision to be healed, it is essential to be sure that such a decision is within the will of God.

It is possible, for example, that a sickness is actually the body's cry for rest. A person laid low with the flu could be suffering the result of stress and overwork. The body may be telling the person to slow down and relax, to recuperate from both the flu and overstimulation. The person's push beyond reasonable limits could be doing more physical damage than any flu would ever do. So deciding to be healed may not involve getting up and walking but rather going to bed.

Another exception to the rule that God wants us all well is that the time may not yet be God's time. Perhaps in His wisdom the Lord is trying to teach something about trust and about resting in Him. Perhaps He wants a person to be quiet and listen and allow healing to come at a later time.

Another exception, which can be difficult for many to accept, is that there is a time to die. In God's plan and according to God's will, there is a time to let go and accept death gracefully as the end of the journey on earth and the passage to the eternal life of heaven. It is wise to recognize that time when it comes.

All this being said, there are times when there seems to be an obstacle to healing. The sick person is not responding to medical help or prayer. Sometimes it seems that something is spiritually wrong.

One block to healing is not deciding to accept it. The person, for some reason, conscious or unconscious, is holding on to the sickness. This may seem strange, but it does happen. Most reasons for holding on to sickness fall into one of four categories.

Why Am I Sick?

First, some people use sickness as a weapon or tool for manipulation. One illustration that comes to mind is the case of a married couple, Frank and Beth. Beth had abandoned Frank for another man. Frank was left alone, feeling rejected and totally bereft. He had always assumed that theirs was a good marriage.

Frank developed cancer soon after Beth left. Seeing Frank in a state of suffering and pain rekindled the feelings Beth once had for him. She returned to him, contrite and wanting to take care of him.

Although Frank suffered greatly and was in a great deal of pain, he subconsciously held on to his sickness. He would not allow himself to be healed because of a deep-rooted but unconscious fear that once he was well, Beth would leave him again. After some counsel and prayer, Frank was secure enough in his relationship with Beth to let go of his cancer. He was healed, and the couple was reconciled.

Another example that comes to mind is that of Lina, whose husband, Peter, had hurt her greatly by his many infidelities. Lina forgave him when he apologized, but Peter always returned to the same behavior.

Peter hoped that once he retired, he and Lina would travel the world together. This was his dream more than hers. They saved for the trip, and he planned extensively for it.

The year Peter retired, Lina became ill with various ailments that the doctors could never quite diagnose. She was in and out of the hospital, undergoing tests and consulting specialists. Peter spent all their money taking care of Lina. The consequence was that they never did travel.

Through prayer and counseling it came to light that Lina was using her ailments to punish her husband for his past infidelities. It was unconscious on her part, but it was very real. When Lina was truly able to forgive, she was healed.

People also hold on to sickness because it provides a good excuse for avoiding responsibility. Someone who feels socially unacceptable might develop a headache when it is time to go out for an evening. A mother or a housewife who does not enjoy homemaking can develop sicknesses that help her avoid the responsibility of taking care of the house and family. No one will blame a sick person for not being present, not doing the same work as others, not living up to expectations. Illness is a perfect excuse for those who seek to escape the pressures of life.

Thirdly, for a lonely person who feels ignored and unloved, sickness can be a way of attracting attention, sympathy, and some semblance of love. It has been noted that the population of a hospital tends to shift during holiday seasons. There are always a number of people who want to go home and be with their families for the holidays, and many of them recover enough to be able to do just that. Yet people without families or those who are in dysfunctional relationships tend to get sick during the holiday season. This can be a desperate cry for attention and sympathy. The power of the subconscious mind, truly mind over matter, is a dynamic that is often at work in sickness and the healing process.

A fourth reason why a person may be unable to release a sickness is that the sickness has become an identity. He or she thinks, "I have always been this way. I will always be like this." "I have always had asthma. I will always have asthma." "I have always had sinus trouble. I always will have sinus trouble." "I always get a cold in December. I will get a cold this December." The person practically embraces illness rather than deciding to stand against it, move beyond it, and accept healing and wholeness.

Some people who have lived with illness for a long time have a difficult time even imagining a healthy life. Sickness can become a familiar home in which to live, with complacent attitudes as to what has always been and what will always be. This is a way of denying faith. Faith can conceive of new realities and can accept God's will for wholeness and life. Yet the positive promise of the Lord to bring life is both an invitation and a challenge.

Yes to Healing, Hope, and Love

Pam was an intelligent young woman who was also very timid. She was never very adventuresome, keeping close to home as she grew up. Going off to college was a traumatic event for Pam. She had never been separated from her parents for more than a day. She disliked living in the dorms, had difficulty adjusting to campus life, made few friends, and was generally unhappy with her situation.

After the Christmas holidays Pam became sick with hepatitis and was forced to withdraw from school and return home. She did not respond to medical help or to prayer for healing. She languished in her ill health.

Through prayer, discernment, and ministry, it became obvious that Pam was unconsciously rejecting healing. If she were healed, Pam would be expected to head back to college. But as a sick person she could remain in her family and be taken care of, and no one would question her situation. Being sick had positive consequences for her.

While praying for healing for Pam, it was important to ask the question, "Do you really want to be well?" This was not done in an aggressive or guilt-inducing way but with kindness and firmness. With love and prayer and encouragement, Pam was healed and ultimately able to move on with her life.

At the pool of Bethesda, Jesus placed the decision to be healed into the hands of the invalid. The man could have responded, "I cannot get up. I cannot walk. I am sick. I am paralyzed. That is impossible." Some faith is necessary to receive healing.

At the very least, faith is the acceptance of Christ's grace and His gift. Faith is openness to what God wants and desires. Christ needs our openness to the future if His work is to be accomplished.

At some point in the healing process, the sick person must accept health, the freedom that health brings, and the responsibility that comes from that freedom. The person must consciously reject sickness as a crutch, an excuse, or an identity and accept the responsibilities life brings. Key to this decision is accepting God's love, which makes life worth living. Two qualities of that love are essential.

One is that God's love is unconditional. It cannot be bought. It cannot be bartered or manipulated. God's love is simply there. His love is present for the worthy and for the unworthy. It is present for the sinner. It is equally present for the sick and for the well. A person needs to be secure in his or her relationship with God before stepping out in health and accepting the responsibilities that health brings.

The second quality of God's love is that it is steadfast — that is, it can never be lost. So if someone walks in health and in freedom and yet fails, stumbles, or falls, God's love is not forfeited. God does not send sickness to punish the sinner. God is not fickle in His love.

Acceptance of God's unconditional love is the foundation for healing and wholeness in life. It is the only real security in this world. It gives peace to the soul, serenity to the mind, and joy to the heart.

And so we pray

Picture a sick person standing before Jesus. Perhaps you are that person. The person leans on a crutch, and the crutch has a name. It is the name of the sickness that afflicts the person. Perhaps it is migraine headache, asthma, ulcer, sinus troubles, or cancer.

The person stands before the Lord, leaning on the crutch, and the Lord asks the same question that He asked the man at the poolside, "Do you really want to be well?"

The person with the crutch might respond, "Lord, I am afraid. I have never been well before. I don't know life without sickness."

The Lord says, "You need have no excuse with Me. You need have no crutch. Lean on Me, and I will be your strength. I will be your support. Understand that I am here. Now you can drop your crutch and come to Me."

The sick person must take that crutch and drop it, leave it behind, and walk to the Lord. The Lord reaches out with His healing touch and says, "Be made whole. Your faith in Me has made you well. You do not need a crutch. You need to lean on nothing but Me. You need no excuses because you have My constant love."

The person, touched by the Lord, receives the healing love and is made well. It is now possible to walk without the crutch, giving joyful thanks to the Lord for the healing.

7

HEALING IN FORGIVENESS

When you stand praying, if you hold
anything against anyone, forgive as your
Father in heaven forgives, and He in turn
will forgive you all your sins.

Mark 11:25

Throughout the Gospels we find a consistent correlation between prayer and forgiveness. Prayer, this intimate life shared between God and the person, is connected to forgiveness by inner necessity. The heart must be clear of resentments and anger if it is to be in union with the Father of mercy and love.

Healing prayer, whether for physical ailments or for inner wounds of the heart and spirit, is interwoven with all the Gospel teachings on forgiveness. Healing prayer cannot be effective if it is blocked by negative attitudes and bitterness in the heart due to unresolved anger. As prayer in faith can affect healing, so forgiveness affects both prayer and healing. In fact, forgiveness lies at the heart of all spirituality.

Jesus as Savior is all about the forgiveness of sin. He is called Jesus because "He will save His people from their sins" (Matthew 1:21). He died on the cross so that sin may be forgiven. This is not a minor, optional issue. This is His identity, the essence of His work, the heart of His ministry.

The Gospel is not simply about forgiveness; the Gospel *is* forgiveness. The Good News is that the dark reality of sin is touched by the grace of pardon and mercy, freely given to the world by a gracious God. Jesus died for the forgiveness of the sins of all: the unworthy, the ungrateful, those who would accept Him and those who would not.

The first responsibility of the Christian who has been forgiven by God is to forgive others. What has been received as a gift must be given as a gift. This flow of grace is a spiritual law.

Healing and forgiveness are connected in two ways. First, resentment and anger can cause physical, emotional, and psychological problems. Many people become sick simply because they are crushed under the weight of their grudges and the desire for revenge.

Many psychiatrists and psychologists would say that emotional problems are in some way caused by unforgiveness. The ancient Greeks called this negativity *bile,* and they saw it as the root cause for many illnesses. The bile made a person bitter and sour in personality and disposition. We all know people who have sunny dispositions and others who are forever angry and resentful.

Secondly, unforgiveness stands as a barrier to the healing power and forgiving love of God. That obstacle can be removed only with a decision to forgive.

Christ commands that we forgive and let go of resentments. On the day He rose from the dead, His first gift to the Church was the imparting of the Holy Spirit, precisely so that His disciples would have the power to forgive: "Receive the Holy Spirit. Whose sins you forgive will be forgiven" (John 20:22–23). The disciples have the freedom to choose pardon over resentment. With freedom always comes responsibility.

When I first began praying for healing, the connection between healing and forgiveness seemed like a theory. One experience brought it to my conscious awareness as a very vital teaching.

We had a weekly Mass and healing prayer at the house where I was stationed at the time. Marilyn came every week for prayer because she was afflicted with cancer and suffered a great deal. She never really got better, but miraculously, she did not get worse, which was against the norm for her type of cancer.

But it always bothered me that Marilyn did not get better, so one day I began to explore this stalemate. I asked her whether she had a need to forgive anyone. Her answer was immediate and strong.

"Yes," she said, "my sister. I hate her with all my heart." The vehemence and bitterness in Marilyn's voice took me aback. I told her that if she wanted to be healed, she would have to forgive her sister. Her answer was, "I would rather have cancer."

That opened a new direction in our weekly prayer. We would pray for the healing of cancer, of course, and then continue to pray for the hurt in Marilyn's heart. We would ask God to give her a desire to forgive, willingness to forgive, and openness to the grace of forgiveness. After many weeks of prayer and conversation, she came to the point of wanting to forgive. However, she still did not want to relate with her sister.

One day just before Christmas, Marilyn said that she had arrived at a decision: She chose to forgive and let go. This announcement came with a flood of tears and emotions; hers was an authentic and heartfelt decision.

After the holidays Marilyn came to our meeting radiant and joyful. Grace and miracles had flowed in her life. The cancer was responding to treatment, and Marilyn was feeling better than she had in many months. More important, her sister had called her over the holidays, and they had had a profound reconciliation.

Scripture tells us that what we bind will be bound and what we free will be freed (see Matthew 18:18). This word came alive in Marilyn's case. The cancer, the relationship, the situation, as well as her own heart were all bound tightly by unforgiveness. Her decision to forgive allowed grace to flow. It was not that God had been absent all those months; the truth is that even His work is bound by unforgiveness and anger.

Two Sides of Forgiveness

Two aspects of forgiveness should be considered. One is that when someone hurts another person, he or she must ask for forgiveness. The other is that the one who has been hurt must forgive.

Now, the first is humanly understandable; the second more difficult to grasp, especially when the one who caused harm does not ask for forgiveness. Yet forgiveness is central to Christian prayers, such as the much-loved Lord's Prayer: "Forgive us our sins, as we forgive those who sin against us" (Matthew 6:12). The Lord's command to forgive is unconditional. He tells us to forgive those who come asking for forgiveness and those who do not.

A person who has been badly hurt may feel entitled to harbor resentment. But Christ demolished any right of that kind when He died on the cross. His death brought about the forgiveness of sin — all sin: my sins against God, others' sins against me, and my sins against others. Jesus takes away any supposed right to harbor resentment, retaliate for a hurt, or nurse a grudge.

With the demolishing of that right, Christ also gives us freedom. No one need be captive to resentment or hate.

Forgiveness is first of all a gift from God, who pardons sinners who otherwise deserve punishment and even death. The gift of forgiveness is the grace that stands at the foundation of all spiritual life. In that gift of forgiveness, given by Christ and freely shared, lies the key to inner freedom and healing.

An important difference exists between forgiveness and reconciliation. Only one person is involved in the act of forgiveness — the one who needs to forgive. Two people are involved in the act of reconciliation: one person forgives, and the other person receives the forgiveness. Forgiveness given and forgiveness received bring about reconciliation between two people who were in some way estranged.

Sometimes it is not possible to have the two principal people involved. Perhaps one has passed away or is somehow not available. Perhaps more hurt and confusion would be caused from an attempted reconciliation. Perhaps contacting the other person would simply not be wise. Still, forgiveness is essential, so it is important to understand this well.

Forgiveness is an act of the will, a decision to let go of a hurt. It is a choice of forgiving over resenting. Whether the other person acknowledges wrongdoing or not, the person who chooses to forgive frees his or her own heart from anger and bitterness and finds wholeness spiritually and as a person of integrity. With forgiveness come peace and wholeness. The forgiving heart is free to love in a way that an angry heart cannot.

Many people carry resentments deep down inside for a long time — against teachers in grade school, classmates, neighbors, parents, or children. Long after others have forgotten an incident, some people still harbor anger and a desire for revenge. These things affect a person's health and well-being. The Lord commands that we release the anger, renounce resentment, and move on to human wholeness.

How Can I Forgive?

To speak of forgiveness can be easy. To actually forgive can be difficult and sometimes seemingly impossible. Some hurts are so truly unjust and so deep that it is almost beyond human ability to speak out words of forgiveness. This, sadly, can be part of the human condition.

In this context several Scriptures take on a new meaning. When Jesus comes into the Upper Room on the day of the Resurrection, He meets the apostles. He breathes upon them, bestowing on them the gift of the Holy Spirit. He says, "Receive the Holy Spirit. Whose sins you shall forgive, they are forgiven them. Whose sins you shall retain they are retained" (John 20:22–23).

In giving the Church the Sacrament of Reconciliation, Jesus gives the power of the Spirit to love and to forgive. He tells us all, "I give you the choice. Whose sins you forgive, they are forgiven. Whose sins you hold onto will be retained. Now, however, you have within you, not of your own human capacity, but by the power of My Spirit, the capability to decide and to choose. If you choose to let go and forgive a sin committed against you, then it will be forgiven. It will be dissolved. But if you choose to hold on to a sin, to harbor a grudge and nurse resentment, then it shall be held bound. The choice is yours." Forgiveness is an act of the will; it is not a feeling, nor is it an emotion.

Some hurts are so deep that it takes more than a little time to overcome the feelings that accompany them. But one can still choose to forgive; one can will to forgive. The Holy Spirit comes to "help us in our weakness," as St. Paul reminds us (Romans 8:26). If there is at least the desire to forgive, the Lord will honor that.

Sometimes the best a person can do is try. She or he can at least say, "I want to forgive, although I cannot right now." The Lord will honor that, because it is an honest response of the heart.

Some years ago I was ministering in Guatemala, up in the high mountains where poor, simple country people live in small villages. Guatemala had just come out of a decades-long civil war, in which many people were killed and many injustices were committed. Stories of atrocities were common.

The people of one village asked for special prayer for healing because of an incident during the war. Many from their village — men, women, and children — had been lured into a trap and attacked. Scores were dead, and dozens were wounded. The people in the neighboring village were largely responsible, acting out of long-standing animosities that had nothing to do with the war. A dozen years later, scars and terrible open wounds were still in the survivors' hearts.

Yet their prayer and desire that day was to be able to forgive so that they could heal and could love and live again. It was a very emotional afternoon as they struggled to find a place in their hearts where the Holy Spirit could work and give birth to forgiveness and reconciliation. The original fear was that forgiving would be seen as weakness, capitulation, and injustice to the ones who had died and to the injured survivors. What all came to understand was that forgiveness is not weakness but the deepest strength and the greatest power and maturity and the only way to heal. I still remember those people in Guatemala as spiritual giants whenever I think of forgiveness.

Jesus' suffering on the cross was the most unjust hurt of all. He was the ultimate victim, the innocent one who suffered physically and emotionally. All the pain of humanity was gathered into His heart. He endured great physical pain; He was misunderstood, unjustly condemned, mocked, and abandoned. All around Him on Calvary were people who hated Him, while many upon whom He should have been able to rely, His disciples and close friends, were not there.

Jesus can understand the anguish and pain of the human heart, for He shared in it. Jesus is the advocate of the many people in the world who are deeply wounded. He understands when no one else does. He is their companion in pain. The man of sorrow and suffering belongs to the whole human race by a special bond of compassion and understanding.

Jesus taught the way of victory over suffering. Coming from Calvary is the power that every wounded person needs to know in order to rise above the pain and find peace and healing. Jesus prayed, "Father, forgive them, they know not what they do" (Luke 23:34). In that prayer is both an important lesson and a profound teaching.

Notice that Jesus did not say, "I forgive them," but, "Father, forgive them." Maybe Jesus was so badly wounded in His heart that it was beyond Him to speak out forgiveness to those people. Perhaps words of forgiveness could never be adequate to the injustice. He simply said, "You forgive them, Father, and I will say Amen. I say yes to the Father's forgiveness."

Then Jesus added, "They know not what they do." This is the gift of understanding, for which everyone who struggles to forgive must pray. Most people who cause pain and hurt to others are actually bound up in their own hurts. They do not understand what they are doing or realize the effects of their actions. It is a truism that "hurt people hurt others."

Everyone who searches for a way to forgive needs to acknowledge the hurt that blinds the offending person and causes him or her to hurt others. It is important also to remember that God knows and understands what no one else sees or understands. God sees the heart, understands the woundedness of people, and forgives all things. To have the heart of Jesus is to be able to see the wounds in the heart of the other.

And so we pray

This prayer will call for the use of the active imagination. Be comfortable and peaceful. Follow the prayer slowly in the quiet of your heart. Verbalize the words as they need to be spoken.

In your mind's eye see a person who caused you hurt or pain. Then see Jesus standing there with you both. Jesus puts His arm around you, and He puts His other arm over the shoulder of the one who hurt you. Standing next to Jesus now, look at that person who has hurt you. Realize that Jesus has a deep love and compassion for you both.

Ask the Lord Jesus to give you His eyes with which to see that person. Ask Him to give you His heart with which to love that person. Ask Him to give you His Spirit with which to forgive the person. Ask Jesus to anoint you with a gift of understanding so that you can look at that person with compassion for his or her own hurts, sorrows, and disappointments. Ask that you would have deep understanding in your heart for that person and a profound compassion.

Then imagine that Jesus, with His arms around both of you, communicates that sense of compassion. You begin to see that person through the eyes of Christ and feel for that person exactly what the Lord Himself feels. You have new insight and understanding and love. You see the other one as a hurting soul, hurting as much as, or maybe more than, you. Jesus says to you, "I know the pain you have suffered. But I am asking, 'Will you forgive? Will you join me in forgiving this person for what has been done to you? It is your decision.'"

It is important to verbalize forgiving words and to picture that person and Jesus beside you as you speak those words:

> *I forgive you. I want to let go of the hurt. I want to let go of the anger. I reject all desire for revenge, and I forgive you. I truly forgive you with the forgiveness of God. I truly forgive you with the very Spirit of Jesus Himself.*

Jesus embraces you both with great love, and you notice His tears. Jesus feels your hurt and the hurt of the other person. He wants you both to find forgiveness, healing, and peace. Now you have opened the way to make that possible. You have pleased His heart, and He says, "Thank you for the words of freedom you just spoke, even after all the pain that you suffered. I am proud of you, and I tell you again that I love you, my child."

8

GETTING FREE OF GUILT

Have mercy on me, O God,
   according to Your merciful love;
according to Your abundant mercy blot out
   my transgressions.
Wash me thoroughly from my iniquity,
and cleanse me from my sin!

For I know my transgressions,
   and my sin is ever before me.

Psalm 51:1–3

One of the questions often asked about healing is why some people are healed and others are not. To some extent we are dealing with deep mystery, and there are no definitive answers to the work of grace. However, experience has taught that guilt can be a stubborn obstacle to the working of grace.

It is common to find people who feel that their sin has brought on sickness as a punishment or who feel unworthy to receive healing because of past sins. These people feel that they deserve to suffer. Even as prayer is offered for healing, they reject healing grace because of guilt.

It is often said that the hardest person to forgive is oneself. Long after God and other people have forgiven someone's sins, the person carries them still, heavy in the heart, like a dead weight that destroys joy and robs peace from the soul. Guilt is one of the subtlest forms of destruction in a person's life. It is nagging. It is burdensome. It can be a major obstacle to healing.

Guilt can even be a cause of sickness or at least be a major contributing factor. A vivid example comes to mind.

A man I'll call Gerry had a severe kidney disorder whose origin and treatment baffled his doctors. Many years before, Gerry's wife had left him for another man, and he had hated her for it. When she became pregnant by the other man, Gerry actually prayed that her child would be born deformed. When the child was born with defective kidneys, Gerry's reaction was one of happiness and even glee.

For over ten years Gerry watched with depraved satisfaction as the couple spent money, time, and effort and were consumed by anxieties and fears for their child. But in the past year, he had begun to recognize the tremendous horror of his deed. Gerry realized that he had actually wished evil on a person. He believed that he might have caused the child's sickness and his ex-wife's distress. Guilt began to grow, and within a year he came down with a severe kidney disorder himself.

Gerry came to grips with the darkness within his own heart. He sought forgiveness from his former wife and her boy. He made up with them as much as he humanly could. He also had to forgive himself. He accepted the Lord's forgiveness and surrendered the past to the Lord's mercy.

As the guilt was healed, the sickness in his kidneys disappeared. Gerry was healed, in fact, without even praying for that healing.

Flavors of Guilt

Guilt itself is good and necessary to the human makeup. Guilt motivates people to repent after doing something wrong. It moves people to repair the harm they caused. The absence of guilt in the face of wrongdoing speaks of a deficient conscience and lack of morality. A psychopath is someone who has no guilt.

To carry guilt past the point where it has served its purpose, however, becomes more destructive than helpful. Some people retain a bondage to guilt rather than accept the freedom that forgiveness brings to the heart. When guilt lives on in a person after the point of repentance and forgiveness, it no longer serves a positive purpose. Rather it becomes toxic; it becomes a destructive emotion that steals life from the soul. Positively, guilt spurs the person to turn to God seeking forgiveness; negatively, guilt blocks the person from receiving full forgiveness.

Several kinds or degrees of guilt need to be considered. Most common is a certain "floating" guilt that does not attach itself to any particular memory or experience. It is an all-pervasive sense of unworthiness that the person carries, far beyond anything that can be concretely identified as sinful behavior. The person thinks that he or she deserves to be sick, deserves to suffer, and is unworthy of being healed and experiencing the joy of life.

That feeling can give rise to the thought that God is a God who punishes. He is perceived as strict, demanding, and exacting — a God who constantly needs to be appeased and who is never pleased with the meager efforts that one makes to honor Him. Repentance and penance are considered ultimately inadequate, since God is always angry with a sinful people who cannot live up to the high standards of holiness He sets.

Another common and obvious kind of guilt is for actual sins committed. Sin is more than a mistake or an error in judgment; sin is an offense against God, the breaking of one of His commandments. Many people are burdened by shame, self-recrimination, and self-condemnation as a result of a time of sin or some act of sin. They experience a nagging sense of guilt that simply does not go away. The person may be more aware of a need to be punished than of the need to be forgiven.

Several years ago I preached and ministered at a maximum security prison. One person there taught me something about guilt and forgiveness. John was doing major time, as they say. The fact that he was sentenced to twenty-five years to life in a maximum security prison says a lot about his criminal activities.

John told me that at the beginning of his time in the prison, he was on the verge of insanity or suicide. The thoughts of the people he had hurt and the lives he had affected lived in his mind day and night. He could not block them out, and since he was in a prison cell, he had precious few distractions to occupy him. One of his most difficult thoughts was about the shame and embarrassment he had brought to his family. John felt that he was worthless, beyond redemption, a failure and an outcast in this world.

Then John made a Cursillo-style retreat offered to prisoners every year. There he had a major experience of God's mercy. He realized, deeper than words could express, the absolute and unconditional love and forgiveness of God. He was forgiven and washed clean. The prison sentence was justice served, but forgiveness was mercy. John experienced deep healing from the pangs of guilt that had lived in him for years.

John and I corresponded for a few years. He always signed himself "John #76344563, a free man in Christ." And that is how he saw himself. Prison walls and bars could confine him physically, but his heart was free from guilt and condemnation. He was loved by God and redeemed by Jesus Christ; he was a temple of the Holy Spirit. His was a vital and living relationship with God that was beautiful to behold. I always think of John as a living example of healing from guilt and shame and a sign of hope for all who labor under these oppressive yokes.

A more subtle and human guilt comes from failure rather than sin. Failure is not necessarily a sin against God but rather derives from human error, misjudgment, or folly. A person can be burdened by a sense of guilt because of some mistake, especially when it caused harm to someone else. The person might go through life asking, "How could I have been so stupid?" "How could I have been misled like that?" "How could I have made that tragic error?"

Think of someone who causes a fatal accident. This is not a conscious or deliberate act. It may be careless or truly accidental, but it is a failure with tragic consequences that leaves the legacy of guilt. The sense of shame and unworthiness can be the same as if the person had committed some terrible sin. Forgiveness, especially self-forgiveness, is necessary across the whole spectrum of human failure, sinful and otherwise.

A related kind of guilt comes from the sense — whether real, imagined, or exaggerated — that one could have done more, tried harder, and persevered longer. This kind of guilt comes from the feeling of being inadequate. It can be a painful wound in the human spirit that affects a person's self-esteem and ability to experience joy in life.

Think about parents with a problem child. Some parents spend endless hours reliving their parenting experience and listing everything they could have done differently or should not have done at all. (Since no one ever parents perfectly, there will always be a list of mistakes, missteps, and missed opportunities.) This destructive thinking gives birth to toxic guilt in the soul. It is perfectly useless, since nothing can be done over, and assuredly the parents did the best they could in the circumstances. But guilt tends to linger and rob peace and joy from the soul. The guilt can take on a life of its own.

Victory Over Guilt

God has a liberating word: Forgiveness of sin frees people from bondage to guilt and the sense of unworthiness.

> I shall pour clean water over you, and you will be cleansed of your impurities. I shall cleanse you of all your defilements and all your idols. I will give you a new heart, and I will put a new spirit in you. I will remove your heart of stone, and I will give you a heart of flesh instead. With My spirit in you, you will live....
>
> On the day I cleanse you from all your sins, you will know that I, the Lord, have rebuilt what was destroyed.
>
> (Ezekiel 36:25–27, 33)

Scripture tells us that God is a God who forgives. He is a merciful Father more than a stern judge. He loves His people. This scriptural image of a compassionate God is the one we want to root in the hearts and souls of all people.

God has care and compassion for all suffering people, no matter the source of the suffering. God is not a scorekeeper. He is not a God of punishment and condemnation.

He does not deal with us according to our sins,
nor requite us according to our iniquities.
For as the heavens are high above the earth,
so great is his steadfast love toward those who fear him;
as far as the east is from the west,
so far does he remove our transgressions from us.

(Psalm 103:10–12, RSV)

Some people blame God for the feelings of shame and guilt they carry. But people put these burdens on themselves; the burdens do not come from God. People can be harsh, judgmental, mean, and condemning, and they project these qualities onto God. But God is more merciful than people. He has tender compassion. He understands frail humanity. He knows the weakness of the flesh. He demands no more than what can be reasonably given: a repentant heart.

God takes our sins away from us — "as far as the east is from the west" (Psalm 103:12). We need to accept and embrace this forgiveness as pure gift.

Everyone seems to know the famous quote from John 3:16 — "God so loved the world that He gave His only begotten Son." The next verse is less well-known but just as important in understanding the heart of the Gospel. "*Jesus did not come to condemn the world but to save it.*" Indeed, Jesus is the judge of the world. However, in St. Paul's letter to the Hebrews, we are told that He is a merciful judge (see Hebrews 8:12). Jesus came to us in the flesh and experienced the fullness of humanity in all its dimensions. He is able to sympathize with us in our weaknesses because He Himself was tempted in every way we are, even though He is without sin (see Hebrews 4:15). We approach Jesus with confidence because He is merciful and compassionate.

In Jesus we find a compassionate friend who is also our judge. St. Paul sums it up: "For those who are in Christ Jesus there is no condemnation" (Romans 8:1). Redemption is ultimately about freedom from sin and from guilt and recrimination. Forgiveness of sin is a blessed liberation and a true healing of the soul wounded by sin.

Forgiveness is a re-creation. St. Paul, who had his own history of sin and failure, was captivated by the gift of forgiveness. He thought about it and wrote about it extensively in his letters. He tells us that if we are in Christ, we are a new creation. The old order has passed away, and the sins of the past are forgotten (see 2 Corinthians 5:17). The future is more important than the past. The love of God triumphs over the anger of God.

In Christ we are made new and given the new life of grace. Therefore we have no right to hold on to the past or continue to live there. What was tarnished and ruined has been made clean. As often as we turn to God with repentance, He grants forgiveness. It is all grace. It is not earned or deserved; it is gift. Guilt has no place, no role, no reason, and no purpose in the heart of a forgiven sinner.

There is an interesting interplay in the Scripture concerning the very different roles of Satan and Jesus. In the book of Revelation, we read that Satan is the accuser, who day and night accuses the brethren before God (Revelation 12:10). He is like a prosecuting attorney. He points out faults. He calls to mind past failures and sins. Satan reminds both God and man of the true unworthiness of sinful humanity. Satan recalls how very undeserving and how spiritually poverty-stricken humans truly are before God.

However, St. Paul presents Jesus as the intercessor. If Satan is the prosecuting attorney, Jesus is the defense attorney who stands before the Father and pleads humanity's cause (see Romans 8:34; Hebrews 7:25). Jesus died for sin; He shed His blood for us as redemptive sacrifice. For the Lord Jesus there is no sin that forgiveness cannot touch. There is no failure that He does not understand. There is no weakness for which He does not have compassion.

Since we have such a high priest — a forgiving, understanding, and compassionate God — we have no right to hold any sin against anyone, especially ourselves. We have no right to harbor guilt or to accuse ourselves for things that are past. We have to accept the forgiveness, the understanding, the compassion, and the tender love of the Father.

Perhaps down deep there is almost a pride in retaining sin. "My sin is so great and my failure so huge, even God cannot touch it." No sin is so deep that God's love is not deeper still. No guilt is so great that God is not greater still. The only sin to be concerned about is the sin for which we have not repented. Guilt cannot stand before mercy and forgiveness.

And so we pray

Using your vivid imagination, visualize the scene of Jesus washing the feet of His disciples at the Last Supper. Imagine that you are in the group, as Jesus moves from person to person, washing and drying the feet of His followers. Imagine the stunned silence and awe as Jesus kneels before His disciples.

Then picture Jesus kneeling before you and looking up at you. He pours out clean water, living water, pure and life-giving. Give a name to each stain and defilement on your soul. Then watch the stains dissolve as the living waters flow over them. Jesus cleanses you of all defilement — all tarnish, stain, dirt, and filth. He washes you of all your sins.

Jesus removes from you all residue of guilt, shame, and self-condemnation. The cleansing waters refresh your spirit and renew your soul. Allow the Lord Jesus to minister to you. He is healing you, spiritually and physically.

Jesus speaks to you: "I know your past and your sins. You must know that I forgive you."

Lean toward the Lord, look directly into His eyes, and tell Him, "I accept Your forgiveness, and in the spirit of Your love, I forgive myself."

9

OVERCOMING DEPRESSION AND SELF-PITY

The people who walked in darkness
have seen a great light;
on those who lived in deep shadows
a light is now shining.
God makes their gladness great
and their joy increase.
They rejoice now in His presence
as people rejoice at the time of harvest....
For the yoke that was weighing heavy,
the crushing burden they were carrying,
and the rod of the oppressor,
these You break.

Isaiah 9:2–4

Isaiah had a sensitive heart for the sorrows and heartaches of the people. He lived through painful times with the Israelites — war and defeat, occupation and oppression — so he understood the crushing burdens they carried and the near despair in which they lived.

Even as Isaiah acknowledged the dark gloom in which the people wandered, he spoke of salvation and hope, a time of deliverance and freedom. In the passage just quoted, salvation is pictured as a light piercing the darkness and dispelling the shadows of gloom. This is the hope and promise of God: that there is more than darkness and gloom in life; the light gives joy and happiness, and the light will prevail.

Many people who seek healing prayer are walking in darkness, under the gloomy clouds of despair. We may have different problems now, but time and space do not change the fundamental realities of life: Sadness and depression are the lot of many. Problems seem overwhelming and difficulties too much to bear.

Two types of people seem to live in these dark clouds: those who wallow in self-pity and those afflicted with depression. Although these are two different problems, people burdened with them are alike in some ways. People who are depressed often get caught in a morass of self-pity; self-pitying people easily succumb to depression. We will discuss the problems separately and then tie them together.

Poor Me

The self-pitying person seems to be caught up in a web of misfortune. It is what one can call the "poor me" syndrome. This person groans and moans, "Everything is wrong. Everything is always wrong. Everything always happens to me. No one loves me. I am all alone and lonely. Everything in my life is misfortune, bad luck, sadness, failure, brokenness, and sorrow."

In some ways the lament that "no one loves me and no one cares" is almost self-fulfilling. This person often seeks out a sympathetic ear and a shoulder to cry on and then pours out a litany of woes. Friends are burdened by such negativity. No one wants to endure the endless complaining that seems to feed upon itself and drag others down. One might offer positive solutions that the self-pitier only rejects as impossible or unworkable.

The person with self-pity is actually a prisoner to the past. As the person looks back over life's experiences, the accumulated weight of past problems, hurts, bad luck, and failures crushes hope for the future. It seems impossible to imagine good fortune when the past is filled with misfortune.

In the present the person dwells on the negative. He or she takes hold of every problem and sorrow and magnifies it. The result is that the negatives in life block out the positives. Life seems to be devoid of joy and hope. The person's perception becomes reality in the end.

Some people seem to want to live in shadow and despair because of a negative view of self. These people seem to have a need to prove just how bad things are. They feel compelled to tell others about the latest misfortune, the latest sorrow, the latest bit of bad luck. There is almost a tinge of masochism in them, a delight in degrading themselves by dwelling on how bad off they are. Misery is the reality of life that cannot be overcome, so it seems.

In our prayer community some years ago, the ultimate sufferer from self-pity was a woman I will call Kathleen. She was the most negative person I have ever met. If "home on the range" is "where never is heard a discouraging word," Kathleen lived somewhere totally opposite. She saw everything in life as part of a plot against her, a conspiracy to keep her down and deprive her of happiness.

Kathleen was a challenge to me and to the larger community as well. This is not the kind of person who receives prayer and then changes. Recovery requires a persistent and committed ministry. Prayer is the beginning of the ministry, but it must be complemented by listening, counseling, positive reinforcement, encouragement, and patience.

This is a fairly difficult problem to minister to because the person finds it almost impossible to think positively, reject sadness, and accept the love of God. He or she seems incapable of celebrating the presence of God in the world or acknowledging that life is a gift.

The Darkness of Depression

Depression is similar to self-pity in that it seems as though a cloud of gloom hangs over the person and crushes the person under its weight. The will of a person who is depressed seems to be broken by uncontrollable sadness and despair. Life is overwhelming.

If the person with self-pity is a prisoner to the past, the person who is depressed is a prisoner to the future. A person who is truly depressed looks to the tasks of everyday life and the demands of tomorrow and sees them as totally impossible and absolutely overwhelming. Every duty, job, or responsibility is magnified.

For a truly depressed person, simply getting out of bed in the morning requires superhuman effort. Doing the dishes, taking care of the house, going to work — the simplest of tasks — overwhelm to the point that life seems impossible. The depressed person is locked out of the future because he or she finds it impossible to hope for or to even imagine a life of joy.

Depression can be "occasional," such as post-partum depression or depression after a divorce or job loss. It can also be deeply rooted and chemically based. In any situation it is oppressive and destructive. People in every walk of life suffer from it.

Judith was successful in her career and a quite capable person. But when she became depressed, the only thing that mattered was how she felt, and that was always both sad and bad. She could not perform at work nor hold her own in a conversation. Her personal relationships suffered, as did her job and family.

The most difficult thing for Judith was that she could do nothing to help herself, this woman of great competence and ability. Even prayer was too much to ask, because it involved a degree of hope and effort. It was very difficult for her to admit such basic weakness.

While self-pity seeks almost compulsively to share its sadness, depression often seeks isolation. A depressed person becomes more and more locked in and cut off from others. Gloomy clouds of sadness become prison walls that trap the person in bitter loneliness.

Demands of well-meaning people to "snap out of it" and "just go about your daily routine" are not helpful. Depression is not something one chooses and will not easily yield to decisions to simply change one's outlook, however much the person might desire to do so. Such demands only create guilt in the depressed person, and guilt increases the depression. It becomes a downward spiral, a free fall into darkness.

Yet we know that God's will is for joy, not sadness. Throughout Scripture God enjoins us to rejoice, to be glad, and to celebrate.

> Rejoice in the LORD, O you righteous!
> Praise befits the upright.
> Praise the Lord with the lyre,
>   make melody to Him with the harp of ten strings!

Sing to Him a new song,
>   play skillfully on the strings, with loud shouts.
>>   (Psalm 33:1–3; see also Leviticus 23:40; Isaiah 61:10;
>>   Zechariah 9:9; Matthew 5:12)

One of the fruits of the Holy Spirit and the mark of a true Christian is joy (see Galatians 5:22).

The truth is that the healing love of God, ministered in love and gentleness, can pierce any darkness. It brings a sense of security and peace to the person. It brings new hope and engenders life.

Healing Love

For both the person suffering from self-pity and the person suffering from depression, healing is possible. They both need healing love through healing prayer.

There are special demands put upon the minister in both cases. First of all, the decision to be healed is almost too much for the person to make. Visions of tomorrow are colored by dark clouds, and joy seems to be beyond the realm of imagining, beyond the horizon of the person's experience or capacity to receive. The person dares not hope.

Secondly, healing cannot be forced; it may take time to unfold. The healing minister needs to be patient, gentle, and tender, never demanding more of a response than the person can comfortably give. The faith, confidence in the Lord, and quiet trust belong more to the minister than to the depressed or self-pitying person.

At the same time, the minister should seek a response in proportion to what is possible. What the wounded soul can give must be given; what the depressed person is able to achieve must be done. The person must take positive steps but never more than he or she can take at that time.

Prayer for people like Judith and Kathleen must be vivid and optimistic. It needs to be spoken aloud, to be heard clearly by the afflicted person, who cannot articulate a prayer alone. The prayer should look into the future and imagine tomorrow as a new day and a new beginning.

Judith and Kathleen both received healing prayer. Ministry to both was a process requiring long-term commitment to personal involvement and encouragement. I do not know if I would say that they were ever "healed," but life became a lot more tolerable, livable, and blessed because of loving and caring prayer from a community of faith.

And so we pray

This prayer uses the vivid imagination and engages the person through guided imagery. The person receiving ministry listens and follows the prayer by picturing the unfolding images.

The one guiding the prayer might see a cloud blanketing the person with sadness and sorrow, or a weight crushing the person, or a trap holding him or her down in the dust.

The minister thus enters into the world of darkness and shadow and feels compassion for the afflicted one. The minister can see the sadness, despair, and self-pity that control the person's life.

The person being ministered to will find such pictures easy to imagine, as these are images of what life has become. The afflicted person begins to feel understood and accepted as the minister verbalizes the situation.

Now the minister pictures the light of Christ and the light of His love and peace. Just as the fog dissipates under the light of the sun, one can picture that cloud dissipating under the light of Christ. It begins slowly, ever so slowly, to lighten and lift and then disappear.

Finally, the light of the Lord touches the heart of the suffering person. Jesus is beside that person. The light comes from His Sacred Heart. He smiles with love and compassion. He speaks with the understanding of one who truly knows the hurts and sorrows and burdens people carry: "I give you My promise of hope. If you trust Me and let Me work, I will bring you new life."

Jesus takes from His heart a gift of joy and places it in the heart of the hurting person. He says, "The day will come when you will find peace and truly rejoice once again. Life will have a new vitality for you. The world will be less threatening and dark. Colors will be bright and vivid. You will go about your daily life with joy, with singing and gladness in your heart, with psalms of hope and joy upon your lips and praise in your spirit."

The suffering person takes that gift of joy and holds on to it tightly. That promise of God will not fail. The day of joy will come, and it will come soon. There will be new hope. The Lord imparts His blessing. As the person quietly accepts it, His work begins anew.

10

ACCEPTING ONESELF

Lord, it was You who created my inmost self.
It was You who put me together. You shaped
    me, fashioned me, and You Yourself
    created me.
For this great mystery, I thank You.
For the wonder of myself, I thank You.
    For the wonder of all Your works,
    I thank You.
O Lord, You know me through and through.
You watched my bones take shape
as I was being formed in secret
and knitted together in the darkness of the
    womb.

                          Psalm 139:13–15

The psalmist who penned these words celebrates the beautiful work of God that he is. He affirms and celebrates the fact that it was the Lord who personally created him and fashioned him as a unique individual. No one is an accident, a mistake, or an oversight.

"Lord, for the wonder of myself, I thank You." Many people have a problem making that statement. It seems prideful and self-centered to affirm what a wonderful creature I am.

And many say, "I don't like who I am. I don't like the way I look, the way I act, the person I am, and what I have become. I am insignificant and of no account." Some might think such statements indicate humility, but they actually point to a problem with self-acceptance and self-love.

Too often humility has been seen as a way of sanctifying negative attitudes toward oneself, attitudes that are destructive and not in keeping with God's loving acceptance and affirmation of the person. Authentic humility and a positive self-image are quite compatible, and both are necessary for a balanced spirituality. It is important to understand them in the right way.

My experience from years of counseling is that many people simply do not like who they are. While I was teaching and counseling in high school, my students would confide, "I hate myself and wish I were dead." In a less extreme form, "There's something wrong with me. I don't like being me. I don't like who I am. I wish I were more like him," or, "I wish I were more like her." There was no celebration of the fact that each person is a very special gift of God. I always thought it terribly sad that such good people were so lacking in the simple yet necessary gift of self-acceptance.

The amazing and even humorous thing among the students was that the one they envied was often the same one who envied them! A well-known and much-admired basketball player on the school team would confide that all he could do was play basketball, and he wished that he had the intelligence of this student or the social grace of that one. Then one of those very students would come into my office and say that he was envious of that basketball player and his popularity.

Some years ago a study was done among high school students on the question of identity and self-acceptance. One question on the survey asked, "If you could be anyone in the whole world, who would you want to be?" The survey gave several options for answers: saints, politicians, religious figures, movie stars, actors, and so on. The last option offered was "me." Fewer than 10 percent of the students chose to be themselves.

The young can feel that they have little to offer and are not respected or prized by society. This can lead to melancholy, depression, and despair. Among certain youth the mantra is "Tune out and drop out." They feel that no one really cares.

What Am I Worth?

Both individuals and society in general need to contend with the struggle for a sense of worth. We see a Down syndrome child eliminated from the mother's womb to relieve society of the burden of caring for someone who will never contribute. When people grow old, many are shunted into retirement and nursing homes, where they can feel worthless. The message in our consumer world seems to be that people are of value only if they can produce something and earn money.

Self-rejection leads to dissatisfaction — with oneself and with life. It is as though the soul has been wounded and cannot heal. There is an endless and anxious search to be someone or something other than who one already is. While there are legitimate reasons for plastic surgery — such as correction of a cleft palate and other deforming and debilitating defects — it can be an expression of a person's rejection of self and a desire to be someone else.

In the other direction, lack of self-worth can lead to feverish attempts to prove oneself. A person can be driven to make money, accumulate status symbols, and acquire fame.

We speak of a person's being "worth millions," as though the person has a price tag.

Left to grow, self-rejection can lead to self-hatred, which manifests itself in more destructive ways. We see a virtual epidemic of this among young people today — bulimia and anorexia, for example. Some people resort to cutting or mutilating themselves, compulsively inflicting pain as a manifestation of self-hatred. Followed to its logical conclusion, self-hatred sometimes leads to suicide, the ultimate destruction of self.

Love of self can certainly lead to arrogance, and recognition of sinfulness can lead to self-hatred. In fact, we need both truths: We are wonderfully unique creations of a loving Father God, and we are sinful and imperfect at the same time. This is simply the human condition. There are reasons to be proud and reasons to be humble.

To reject oneself because of sin betrays a mistaken understanding of God's merciful love. Jesus told us to love others as we love ourselves (Matthew 22:39). We cannot love others very well unless we love ourselves. To be at peace with oneself is the gateway to peace with the world and a harmonious relationship with God. Accepting and celebrating one's unique goodness and beauty is also a solid foundation for good health.

A man suffering from lupus once came for counseling, prayer, and healing. We prayed for Mark's healing but did not see any positive results. Through counseling we found that Mark had a basic feeling of ill ease with his own personality. He had been adopted, and he had always felt that he had been rejected because there was something wrong with him. This was a feeling that he had internalized to the point where it became his "truth." In his own words, Mark believed that he was "a reject."

One day someone asked Mark to explain the disease of lupus. He said something very revealing: "Lupus is a disease where the body ultimately destroys itself." That description gave us a clue that led us to his ultimate healing. What seemed to be happening was that Mark's self-hatred was working at the physical level; his body was turning against itself.

Through prayer, day after day, Mark fought against feelings of self-rejection and self-hatred. Eventually he came into a true acceptance of his own gifts, his uniqueness, and his personality. He was finally able to say that he loved himself for who he was. He was able to thank God for the gift of his own creation and his own being. With that affirmation from deep in his heart, the healing of lupus began. After two years Mark's disease had completely disappeared. It was a long process that resulted in both physical and emotional healing.

A Unique Creation

We believe in the all-powerful and all-encompassing love of God. We believe above all else that He is Creator. The logical conclusion is to believe that each and every person is created in an act of love.

We are not made out of nothing, however philosophically correct that may be. "Nothing" is not the essence of the soul. We are created out of love. Love is the heart and core of the human being. This follows naturally and logically from the truth of a personal, loving Creator God and Father. He created each person in a unique, personal, and loving way.

God did not simply create people in general or en masse. He created each one as a special work of His hands. He chose the time and place of birth for each one. He chose the family, the parents, and the circumstances for everyone who has ever been created. Nothing about creation is an accident; all came to be by His loving design.

The well-known creation story in Genesis reveals how the plan of God unfolds. His Word created everything that God made. He spoke it, and it was made. He said, "Let there be light" (Genesis 1:3), and there was light. Everything was created by the word of command and by the breath of His mouth, it says in Psalm 33:6. Everything except for one thing: the human race.

The Scriptures tell us that the Lord said, "Let us make man in Our image, after Our likeness" (Genesis 1:26). God bent down, picked up the dust of the earth, and fashioned Adam with His own hands. He breathed the breath of life into what He had made (see Genesis 2:7). Then God took Adam's rib and fashioned Eve from it (Genesis 2:21–22). God was intimately involved in the creation of both the man and the woman. They were not created from a distance or by a word of command but with a personal, loving, and tender touch.

What is true for Adam and Eve is true for every person God creates: Each is made lovingly unique. It is true of you, and it is true of me. This is both gift and grace, pure and simple. And so the psalm sings of the joy and wonder of being created by God. "For the wonder of myself, I thank You."

It is often said that there are two things that God does not make: He does not make junk, and He does not make a mistake. If God created someone, then that person is neither worthless junk nor a mistake. If God wanted somebody else to exist, He would have created that other person. He created the person He wanted at that particular time and in that particular place. St. Paul writes, "We are God's work of art created in Christ Jesus" (Ephesians 2:10). St. Paul understood some essentially important things about God and creation.

First of all, there is a sublime identity that each person has as God's work of art. That is why human beings are worth saving and redeeming. The work of God that each person is can truly be considered a masterpiece of loving design, to be celebrated and cherished. Certainly it is not to be despised or rejected.

Before God ever asked us to have faith in Him, He first had faith in us. He has faith in each and every person that He creates. Deep in the heart of God is a desire that people be everything that He created them to be. His desire is that they grow, mature, and use every gift and talent that He has given so graciously. This is the special blessing that ennobles and enhances all of creation. Each one's beauty contributes to the beauty of the world God made with such care and love.

Jesus in His life and ministry went forth and touched people. He saw with the eye of God His Father. He looked with the gaze of love. With the love that was in His heart, He saw beyond the person's failures, beyond the person's sins. He saw what His Father had so wonderfully and lovingly created. He saw the image of God in each human soul, however tarnished that image had become. He saw all the hopes and possibilities of that person. He grieved for the wounds and brokenness that crippled the giftedness He saw. Then He reached out and touched with healing love. This healing and restoration are the ultimate divine affirmation of the human person as God's creation of love.

The account of Jesus in the garden on the day of the Resurrection is a fascinating story with wonderful insights. The risen Jesus appears to the weeping Mary Magdalene, who does not recognize Him. What I find most interesting in the story is that Jesus speaks one word to her, *Mary*. That simple speaking of her name brings about an immediate response:

Mary Magdalene recognizes Jesus, rushes to Him, and embraces Him.

Why was the speaking of Mary's name so important, and why was that the key to her recognition of Jesus? The answer is in prior pages of Scripture, where we learn that Mary Magdalene had once been inhabited by seven demons (see Luke 8:2). Some have theorized that she was also a prostitute. In any case she was certainly not welcome in pious circles. But Jesus saw not the sinner but the person. He touched Mary's life and changed her. Mary Magdalene went on to become a great saint.

The minister of healing must always see the uniqueness of each and every person. Very often people cannot see it in themselves until someone else affirms it in them. The minister needs to have the eyes and heart of Christ and be able to say sincerely, "You are a beautiful work of God. You are God's work of creation, special to Him and to me. You are lovable." Jesus wants to call forth and affirm everything that the Father has created the person to be.

And so we pray

Begin this prayer by imagining Jesus standing before you. Picture Him looking into your eyes with compassion and deep understanding. You know that He loves you, and you realize that He knows you intimately and completely. Jesus speaks one word to you: He calls you by your name.

Then the Lord reaches out and puts His hand upon your shoulder. He says, "I bless you, and I celebrate especially that most sacred moment of your life, the moment when my Father created you. The Father called you by name and created you unique and special in all His creation. He created you to be you. I bless that very moment when He placed you as a gift within your mother's womb."

Move forward about nine months, and ask Jesus to bless the day of your birth. The day you entered this world was a very special day for His Father. Jesus tenderly holds you in His arms and thanks the Father for the very special gift that you are. With David the psalmist pray, "I thank You, Father, for the gift of myself, for the gift of who I am. I thank You, Father."

11

BUILDING
SELF-ESTEEM

One day you will finally understand that I
am in my Father, you are in Me, and I am
in you. If anyone loves me, he will keep
My word. My Father will love him, and We
will come to him. We will make our home
within him.

John 14:20–21

Jesus speaks these words to His disciples at the Last Supper.
They are part of the final discourse, the last words He will
speak to them. He summarizes the most important truths
that He wants them to remember as the very foundation of
their faith.

What is so special about these words of Jesus is the affirmation that He and the Father have a deep desire to make
their home within the hearts of the disciples. There is something very special, tender, and warm about that word *home*.
It connotes a sense of belonging, a place where somebody is
comfortable and wants to be. Jesus says that His home — the
place where He belongs and the place where He wants to be
— is within the heart of each believer. He desires to dwell in,
not just visit or touch, the heart of each of His disciples.

Here is a tremendous and overwhelming affirmation of the dignity of a Christian. The Lord of heaven and earth, the all-powerful ruler of the universe, is pleased to make His home within us and among us. This is a truth that everyone needs to hear and understand, especially in our day.

Low self-esteem can become a prison of self-imposed isolation. In one prayer community to which I belonged, there were people who always sat in the back and said little, not because of fear of involvement but because of the sense that they had nothing to offer. My observation was that these people usually had a great deal to offer. They tended to minimize their gifts and put themselves down. They needed to be drawn out and included and their contributions celebrated. They also needed to be encouraged to ask for prayer.

We also find the exact opposite: people who come for healing prayer every time it is offered. They make incessant demands on ministers for more time and more attention. This seems to be a pathetic attempt to show that they are really worth something. Some people need a great deal of affirmation from others because they have so little affirmation themselves. For a brief moment, with a prayer team standing around, that person is the center of attention. This always reminds me of the lost sheep, which must have felt truly valued when the shepherd ignored the other sheep and sought it out (see Luke 15:4–7).

I clearly remember a homeless woman who would come to the prayer community on occasion. More than once I sat with her for a cup of coffee and listened to her story. One thing that sticks in my memory is her thoughts on being committed to a psychiatric hospital. Maria's life was so desperate that a psychiatrist's attention was affirmation for her.

"Imagine," she would say, "some fancy doctor with big degrees, who drives an expensive car, comes and spends time with me, listening and asking me questions. He stops everything he is doing when I am there. He actually spends time with me, and I get to go into his office and everything."

Some who come for ministry are not really looking for healing but only for an affirmation that they are worth something. They are worth someone's time and effort. In fact, some really do not want to be healed: If they get better they might lose their golden opportunity to feel important and loved through ministry! The need for love is deeper than the need for physical healing. The physical need can be obvious, the inner pain more subtle.

Some people suffering from low self-esteem truly believe that healing can happen — but only for everyone else. They tend to say, "God can't be bothered with me, because I am simply not worth it. I am a sinner and unworthy and do not count, so do not waste time on me."

Roots

When we realize the widespread phenomenon of people who do not believe in themselves, who feel they are burdens, who feel useless, hopeless, and without worth or dignity, we need to ask where these feelings came from. The roots of these feelings can be deep, complex, and multiple. It is possible to touch on only a few here.

Our society sometimes reduces people to numbers and commodities. Calling a corporation, such as the phone company, or a government office can make one feel like a number matched with a machine rather than a person with legitimate needs. Good and loyal workers toil for years with a firm only to be terminated suddenly at the whim of a distant executive who sees only the bottom line. The message is loud and clear that the person is not valued.

Parents might tell children that they were unwanted or unplanned, that they came too soon or were born too late. Or they say, "Why can't you be like your brother? Why can't you be like your sister? Why aren't you like the neighbors' children? They are so good. They are so neat. They are so smart. They are so talented, and you are not." Teachers sometimes tell children that they will never amount to anything.

These kinds of statements can come in anger or in jest or maybe even as misguided attempts at discipline. The ideas are planted and remembered and give birth to feelings of shame and insecurity.

I once knew a woman named Rosalind who came for healing prayer. She had what the psychiatrist called floating anxiety, a dark and ever present sense of hopelessness. Rosalind went from psychologist to psychiatrist to counselor and tried various therapies. Nothing and no one seemed to help.

The feelings of despair could be traced back to one moment in her life. Her mother, in a moment of anger, told Rosalind that she had attempted to abort her but the procedure had failed. Rosalind felt that she was rejected, unwanted, a burden, and a mistake.

Prayer was able to heal Rosalind. She received the affirmation and embrace of the One who created her, the One who would never reject her. She experienced the power of God's unconditional love.

The truth is that each person is important to God. He has a tender and fatherly care for every single person He creates. He does not love humanity in the abstract; He loves each person individually. He knows each and calls each one by name. No one is a stranger to Him.

Jesus stands as the ultimate example of one who was secure in His relationship with the Father. Through all of His passion and agony He was not destroyed. His life's work was seemingly in shambles. His friends had deserted Him. Yet He stood self-possessed, with a sense of peace. He was loved by His Father, and His Father would not abandon Him. Nothing else mattered.

Just as with Jesus, our relationship of love to the Father defines our life, dignity, and identity. The truth of that love is eternal, but it needs to be affirmed to become a life-giving reality. It is a truth that must engage the mind and heart and soul.

When the angel Gabriel appears to Mary, he says, "Rejoice. You are highly favored. The Lord is with you" (Luke 1:28). Yet the very next line tells us that Mary did not rejoice at all. Rather she "was deeply troubled on hearing these words" (Luke 1:29). If the Blessed Mother had a difficult time accepting the message of affirming love, we should not be surprised that we all would as well. Hers was a very human reaction.

As the story unfolds in the chapter, we next see Mary traveling to visit her cousin Elizabeth. When Elizabeth greets Mary, she basically speaks the same message that the angel had spoken. "Blessed are you among women…. The mother of my Lord has come to me…. You are blessed because you believed" (Luke 1: 42, 43, 45). It is at that moment that Mary does what the angel told her to do: She rejoices. She sings the hymn we call the *Magnificat*, "My soul praises the Lord, and my spirit rejoices in God my Savior" (Luke 1:46–47). Even though Mary had heard the word of God from the angel, it was not until Elizabeth affirmed that word that Mary could truly rejoice. She had human affirmation of the truth. She finally knew, in more than an intellectual way, that the word was true and that the Lord really did love her in a special way. The minister of healing will make every effort to affirm people in their special relationship to God. What Mary learned and Jesus knew, each one of us must understand and come to know. God personally loves each of His children. Each one of us is unique, blessed, and specially cherished by God.

Remember the teaching of the Church throughout the ages: If you were the only person ever to accept it, Jesus would have died just for you. If you asked Jesus, "Why? Why would you die for me?" He would respond, "You are worth it to Me." This is the greatest affirmation of personal value, worth, and dignity on the planet. Jesus thinks that you are worth dying for.

In chapter 17 of John, Jesus prays, "Father may they be one. May they be one so that the world may believe it was You who sent Me." Then very importantly, Jesus adds, "so that they would come to believe that You have loved them just as much as You loved Me" (John 17:21, 23).

God loves you just as much as He loves Jesus! If He had to, He would not be able to choose between you and Jesus. If we can accept that truth as the very foundation of our lives and our identity, we can have a true sense of our dignity, value, and worth. We have been created in love. We were made in the image and likeness of God and redeemed at a great price. Each of us is precious and valued.

And so we pray

We hear the Lord speak soft and tender words. He speaks to you and to you alone: "You are precious in My eyes. You are special to Me, and I love you."

Here is true rest and peace for your human heart. You are loved with a love beyond all telling. It is gift, and it is grace.

Jesus, I thank You for this love and for accepting me just as I am, even though I am a sinner. You love me and gave

up Your life for me. You must think that I am very valuable and worthwhile. You see not just my sin and failures
but the image of the Father in me. I am created in love
and for love.

Only in You will I ever be at home, and You have
found a home in me. In You I am complete and whole.
Let me experience Your life and love in the deepest part
of my soul. Remain with me, stay with me, and keep me
always close to Your heart. Never let me stray from You,
because in You I have found my peace, my dignity, and
my life.

12

OVERCOMING
ANXIETY

I tell you, do not worry about your life. Do
not worry about what you will eat or drink,
about your body and what you will wear. Is
not your life more important than food? Is
not your body more important than clothes?
Look at the birds in the sky. They do not sow,
they do not reap, nor do they store food in
barns. Yet your heavenly Father feeds them
all. Are you not so much more valuable than
they? Who of you, for all your worrying, can
add one single hour to his span of life? Why
then do you worry about your clothes? See
how the lilies of the field grow. They do not
labor. They do not spin. Yet I tell you that
not even Solomon in all his splendor was
dressed like one of these. Now if that is how
God clothes the grass of the field, which is
here today and tomorrow is thrown into the
fire, will He not much more clothe you? O
you of little faith. Stop your worrying. Stop
saying, "What shall we eat?" or "What shall

we drink?" or "What shall we wear?" It is
the pagans who run after these things. Your
heavenly Father knows what you need. For
you then, seek first His kingdom and His
righteousness, and all these things will be
given to you as well.

Matthew 6:25–27

The Sermon on the Mount is a beautiful and sensitive compilation of the most important and essential points of Jesus' doctrine and spirituality. Included in the sermon are these beautiful words about the loving care and providence of the Father. Because there is a heavenly Father who loves all His children, it is logical to trust rather than to worry or fear.

Jesus would say that one of the first gifts, and an earmark of a disciple, is the gift of peace. "Do not be afraid. Peace" is the most consistent message in the Gospel. When Jesus appears in the midst of a stormy lake and walks on water, He says to the apostles, "Do not fear," and He imparts peace (Matthew 14:25–27). At the Transfiguration on Mount Tabor, He says to the three apostles, "Do not fear. Be at peace" (Matthew 17:1–7). To the father of a troubled child He says, "Fear is useless" (Luke 8:50). After the Resurrection, again, "Peace be with you" (John 20:19, 21, 26).

The teaching of peace is not just a message. It is more than an exhortation or command. It is a gift. God is Father, and He loves us and cares about us — no matter what the external circumstances of life are.

The Rat Race

In contrast to this Gospel gift of peace, we see in our society a huge problem of anxiety and stress. One of the most commonly prescribed medicines today is some form of tranquilizer or sleeping pill. Tensions and anxieties seem epidemic, bringing with them a whole host of medical issues: ulcers, heart attacks, muscle spasms, migraines, intestinal problems, and skin diseases.

I'd like to mention two basic sources of anxiety and tension. The first is society itself. We live in a competitive culture and a consumer society. In common language it is sometimes called the "rat race." There is the need to get ahead or stay afloat, to keep going and to achieve, to earn, to amass, to expand, and to produce. Society is not kind to people.

Life has become unnecessarily complicated with so-called needs, which seem to be newly created on a regular basis. Our dependence on gadgets and devices was unheard of a generation ago. We have a variety of ways to make coffee and dozens of small machines to help prepare meals. What begins as a novelty quickly becomes a necessity. In the end, life becomes encumbered with too many things that obscure their very purpose, which is to simplify life!

I know a man I'll call Ernie, a candidate for a heart attack if ever there was one, who went into his bathroom one morning and noticed the maze of electrical cords. His toothbrush had to be plugged in. His shaving cream had to be warmed. Even his comb had a plug. Life had become unnecessarily complicated.

Ernie thought about what he was really trying to achieve in life. He wanted his life to be defined by what is truly important. His relationship to God was a primary concern, not an afterthought. From that day on he tried to simplify his life.

He wanted to live in a more relaxed and harmonious balance with nature, meeting his needs yet resisting the desires that the consumer society was trying to foist on him.

A Christian can have peace in a way quite different from what the material world offers. Gospel peace is based on a relationship with God, not on material things. The Church's blessing of a newly married couple at a wedding is that the "desire for material possessions would never dominate your lives." This is great wisdom for a couple about to embark on their life journey together; in fact, it is great wisdom for everyone.

Christians who are truly grounded in the love of God need not be part of the rat race. The nonstop feverish activity can be left to others. God can take care of all of our needs; we can trust Him to look after His children with a tender love.

The Worries of Life

A second source of tension comes in the form of controversies that surround us, demanding our attention and draining our energy. People get caught up emotionally in issues such as war, the environment, and politics. The ordinary give-and-take of relationships can cause stress. Parents worry about their children. Fathers worry about their families. People worry about finances. Children worry about school and their grades.

Then there are those burdens that weigh especially heavy, such as a personal tragedy, a health problem, or a breakdown. Some people experience divorce and the collapse of family life. Attempts to save a situation often come down to nothing more than pathetic efforts to manipulate and control, to play God, to be a savior.

It is helpful to focus on one dimension of a problem — the dimension of personal responsibility. Each person must do his or her part; we are not responsible for other people's decisions and actions.

Numerous therapies attract people who are looking for peace. Dietary supplements and health drinks, meditation techniques, yoga, massages, and hypnosis therapies, plus a whole host of other aids promise to restore balance, relax the nervous system, and provide a good night's sleep. If these fail, some people resort to alcohol, pills, or other drugs.

It is very difficult to achieve a balance between caring and being anxious. Some people will not love deeply because they may lose the other person. Better, it seems, to not love at all than to risk hurt and sorrow.

The expression "worry yourself sick" is well founded in experience. I've already mentioned many physical and mental illnesses that can originate in crushing stress. Yet some people seem to enjoy worrying.

A member of our prayer community worried about anything and everything. Arlene had ulcers and insomnia as well as nervous tension. In conversation one day I pointed out that she had little to worry about. Her children were all healthy and financially stable, if not wealthy, and she had a family that many would envy. Her response was classic, "That is what worries me: It may all change someday." Someone could get sick or be laid off from work. Misunderstandings could destroy good relationships.

Our friend simply could not relax and enjoy the blessings that were hers until she finally had an experience of God's love and was able to truly trust in His providence. Fortunately, after many years of letting anxiety be her daily companion, Arlene knew peace. It was a gift from a loving Father God.

The truth is that we can do only what we are able to do; the rest is beyond our control. But what we cannot change, however painful it might be, does not need to destroy us. In fact, when we truly realize that a situation is outside our ability to change, then we are ready to surrender it to God.

Pathway to Peace

Jesus gives peace as a gift. In fact, one of His titles is the *Prince of Peace.* He wills peace as the hallmark of discipleship with Him: "I give you a peace that the world cannot understand. I give you a peace that no one can take from you" (John 14:27).

Jesus calls us to a deep awareness of His lordship and of the loving Fatherhood of God. One popular song proclaims, "He's got the whole world in His hands." That is real and practical faith, knowing that God is truly loving and all-powerful. Scripture tells us that even the powers of hell tremble before Jesus and must obey Him (see Romans 8:38–40; Philippians 2:9–10).

No situation is outside of God's control. He can never be caught off guard. He has everything in hand. He does not have to play catch up with a world that is spiraling out of control.

God is our Father, a loving and personal God. He knows our situations and needs. He may work in mystery, but His name is love, and He can be trusted. He gives His angels charge to watch over, protect, and care for each and every one (Psalm 91:11; Luke 4:10). He calls us His very own children. In this is peace.

We read in St. Paul's letter to the Romans that the Gospel is "the power of God for the salvation of everyone who believes" (Romans 1:16). This is more than faith in the doctrines of the Church; it is total trust and surrender to the love of God. What we believe with our minds we must put into practice. Then we have nothing to fear. The truth is that my life belongs to God before it is ever mine. A marriage belongs to God before it belongs to the couple. Every family belongs to God; children are His before they are entrusted to their parents. The world, the Church, every parish, and every community belong to God first.

The gift of peace is first of all a *gift*. It is not something that anyone can purchase, achieve, learn, or win. It does not come from a bottle or from a pill. It cannot be wrested from the hands of God. What a person can do is have the right attitude and disposition to receive such a gift, consciously surrendering all anxious situations to the providence of God.

Prayer is a sacred time when we take every burden, every anxiety, and every situation beyond our control and give them all to Jesus. It is a time to remember and proclaim that He is the Lord over everything, especially all that needs redemption and healing. In exchange, the gift of peace settles in the heart and brings a tranquility that can only be born of trust.

There are prayers for peace in every Eucharist:

- "Look not on our sins, but on the faith of your Church, and graciously grant her peace and unity in accordance with your will."
- "Lamb of God, you take away the sins of the world, grant us peace."
- Then we say to one another, "May the peace of the Lord be with you."

One good way of praying for and finding peace is the prayer of praise and thanksgiving. A prayer from the liturgy, the Preface, teaches us about that: "It is truly right and just, our duty and our salvation, always and everywhere to give you thanks, Father most holy." St. Paul says to give thanks to God in every circumstance (see 1 Thessalonians 5:16–18). This affirms the truth that a loving God is in charge and wants only blessings for His children.

And so we pray

Picture the Lord in front of you. Imagine that He is holding the gift of peace in His hands. You want to take that gift from Him, but your hands are filled with too many burdens and anxieties.

The Lord reaches out His hands toward you and says, "Give them all to me." You take each situation, look at it, and name it. Hold it consciously and then give it into the hands of the Lord.

> *Cast your burden on the LORD,*
>   *and He will sustain you;*
> *He will never permit*
>   *the righteous to be moved.*

(Psalm 55:22)

Finally your hands are empty. You have given everything over and know that He is in control, that you are free of those burdens. Then Jesus gives you the gift of peace. Receive it with a grateful heart, and live in the peace that His love has granted. He places it deep within your heart, and no one will steal it from you.

13

HEALING HIDDEN HURTS

All authority in heaven and on earth has been given to Me. Therefore, go now and make disciples of all nations. Remember that I am with you always, even to the very end of the world.

Matthew 28:20

Jesus spoke these words at His final meeting with His disciples before His return to the Father. His last words are both the final revelation of His identity and His final commission to His followers.

Jesus is Lord of heaven and earth. He is all powerful. He possesses all authority. He has absolute dominion over all creation. Everything that exists came to be *through* Him (see John 1:3). He is Emmanuel, God with us forever.

What are His disciples asked to do? Jesus gives them the Great Commission, which is the command to go out and proclaim the Gospel, bringing the whole world under His dominion. Everything is to be subjected to His rule and brought into His Kingdom.

There is much to ponder here and many practical lessons to be drawn from these words. Jesus' disciples are indeed sent on a noble task, but they are not sent to conquer the world alone. Anyone who ministers in Jesus' name is not alone at all. The one called Emmanuel is always present.

Wherever Jesus rules, where His Kingdom is established, there is peace, order, harmony, and wholeness. Where Jesus is not acknowledged or recognized as Lord, where God is excluded, there will necessarily be disintegration, conflict, and confusion. To submit all things to His rule is to bring about healing at its deepest level. Healing prayer is about bringing the active dominion of Jesus Christ to bear on every sickness, brokenness, and pain. Jesus embraces and transforms every conceivable aspect of life.

One of the most exciting dimensions of the healing ministry, and one that is beginning to be understood more fully, is the healing of the negative experiences of life, the painful memories that people carry in their hearts. This is an actual healing of the past.

God With Us

As I mentioned in chapter 5, the past cannot be changed, but the way that the past is experienced and remembered can be different. It is the memories of the past, often colored by emotions, that have power to affect people's attitudes, feelings, and reactions, for better or worse. Hurtful and traumatic memories can lie buried in the depths of the heart. Yet healing can touch wherever there is suffering or sorrow.

Jesus is present now and has always been present, even at the dark and painful moments of life. Rather than speak of the absence of God or the silence of Jesus, it is more accurate to speak of His presence that was not experienced or acknowledged at certain times. Since the spirit is not bound by time and space, we are free to recover experiences of years ago and embrace the truth that He was present, even though He was not visible, realized, or acknowledged. And this can bring healing.

Psychiatrists know that even before birth, the emotional climate surrounding a child can leave either a positive imprint or a negative scar. The physical and emotional states of both mother and father, and in fact all the events and experiences surrounding conception and pregnancy, have an effect on the infant. It is important to emphasize that no one is determined by early experiences. However, everyone is profoundly influenced by them.

It makes a difference, for example, whether a person was conceived in love or in anger, fear, revenge, deceit, or even an act of violence. It makes a difference how a mother received the news of the conception. Was the reaction one of delight or one of horrific fear? Was the father's reaction one of acceptance or rejection? The reaction of the people around the parents matters, because that contributed to the emotional climate for both parents and child.

Was the pregnancy thought of as a joy and a gift or an unwanted burden, an unfortunate accident? Was the infant carried peacefully and lovingly over nine months, or were they nine months of anxiety, fear, and nervous tension? Did the mother hold her newborn child, or was the infant taken away and placed in an incubator for days or even weeks before being held by mother and father? When the child was brought home, was he or she welcomed with joy or with stress and tension? Was there an atmosphere of joyful acceptance in the home, or was there sibling rivalry?

Psychiatrists and psychologists can identify, study, and label emotional scars; they can even help people accept reality, cope, and adjust to life. The healing ministry, however, brings the love of Jesus Christ to human brokenness.

The Spirit of God touches the human spirit with love and compassion. He takes what is negative and painful and transforms from inside. No one need be victim to memories that are locked within the subconscious mind.

The healing ministry, especially in its dimension of inner healing, realizes in a positive way that the promise of Jesus is that He is always present. He was the same Lord yesterday as He is today and will be forever. He is the Alpha and the Omega, the beginning and the end (Revelation 1:8; 21:6; 22:13). He loves, and He redeems. The awareness of Jesus' presence is healing in itself.

Psalm 139 states that there is no place to go to escape the presence of the Lord (Psalm 139:7–12). There is no darkness so dark that it can blot out His presence, no hiding place so deep that His love cannot reach, no place so distant that He does not follow. His light can shine in any darkness. His love can touch any depths. He needs, however, to be invited in and acknowledged in some conscious and free way.

New Memories

Memories can be recaptured and recast in a new light when Jesus is consciously brought into them. By using the active imagination, one can relive every moment of life from conception onward, introducing the active and living presence of Jesus into the memory. Jesus' light can illumine the darkness of the past, and His love can flood every moment of our life, past and present.

When the memory has been bathed in love and in light, it loses its ability to influence the present in negative ways. The memory is healed.

One of the first times I had the occasion to pray like this happened almost by accident, but I believe the Lord ordained it in order to teach me some things. Several of us in the healing ministry would read books and listen to teaching tapes and then meet to discuss what we were learning. One particular night we were discussing prayer that would touch negative memories that still affected people's lives. A woman I'll call Marge volunteered that her situation would warrant such prayer.

Marge suffered from what doctors call separation anxiety. She would become agitated and nervous when she thought she was alone or was going to be left alone. She needed constant reassurance that someone was present with her and for her.

It all seemed to stem from an experience when she was about six years old. Marge was quietly taking a nap. Her father was at work, and her brothers were out playing sports. Her mother had to run a quick errand. She would not be gone long.

As seems to happen in these cases, Marge woke up to find the house empty. She ran around the house, going from room to room, but found no one. She panicked and began to weep. She felt abandoned and afraid. When her mother returned a few minutes later, Marge was inconsolable.

This simple experience colored Marge's life. She still remembered her fear years later. She made it a point to try never to be alone again.

None of us had ever prayed for healing of memories, but we were open to learning what the Lord would teach us. We gathered around Marge and entered into prayer. The Lord opened for her a visual image, using her own active imagination.

Marge pictured herself at home at the time of the incident. She could vividly remember the house, her room, and lying down to take a nap. Then she remembered waking up and finding the house empty. She recalled fearfully running through the house looking for someone.

This is where the trauma began in her memory, but this time it was transformed. This time she found Jesus sitting in the kitchen. He quietly greeted her with a smile and asked her to sit with Him while waiting for her mother to get back. He asked her if she would like a cookie, and they sat together at the table talking of many things together. Jesus told her that He is always with her and was there that day too, but she was too upset to notice. He spoke of His love for her and His understanding of all her fears and anxieties. When her mother came back, He sent her to the door to greet her. Marge embraced her mother and told her of her fear and asked her not to abandon her again.

There was a deep healing in Marge's heart and soul that day. The fear and separation anxiety were lessened to a significant degree. She had only to recall the presence of Emmanuel, God with us, to stay calm and at peace where once she would have panicked. In a way the memory was the same, but the presence of Jesus, explicitly recognized, voided the negative consequences. The Spirit of Jesus led the prayer and unfolded the scenario.

Everyone has had traumatic moments and carries scary memories. Perhaps these still cause anxiety. Through healing prayer there can be a new experience of a traumatic event with the warm embrace and secure love of Christ that brings healing. Bringing the past to prayer is not difficult or complicated. What follows is an example of the type of prayer that could be used.

And so we pray

Jesus is with you now. His presence is a very secure presence. His presence is a loving presence. He accepts you, and

He protects you. He knows your heart and all its secrets. He loves you as you are.

You know that if you are focused on the Lord's presence, then nothing can harm your spirit or disturb your peace. Nothing can wound your soul, because the Lord is with you. His love is peace and security and so brings you serenity.

I now ask the Lord to hold you in His arms. Picturing Jesus with His arms around you, you can feel His warm and loving embrace. You know the security of being held in His arms. You can look into His eyes and see the deep love and compassion that He has for you. He knows all your hurts and fears.

You need to know that Jesus was with you from the very beginning of your life. I ask that His light, warmth, and deep compassionate presence would bathe the most holy and sacred moment when you were created. He thanks His Father for creating you. He joyfully blesses that moment when you came into existence. He watches lovingly and with delight as one small cell begins its life.

I ask the Lord, by His presence and love, to touch anything negative that could have surrounded that moment of your conception. I ask the Lord to touch any fear, deceit, anxiety, or anger that may have marred the sacredness of the moment. I ask the Lord to heal any influence on that one small cell that is not goodness or love. His love brings healing to anything less than the wholeness of life-giving love.

The Lord watches as you develop from one cell into an embryo and then a fetus. You are with Jesus, watching yourself grow and develop.

At a crucial moment your mother realizes that she is carrying a child. I ask the Lord to heal any hurtful effects of her nervousness or fears. I ask the Lord to heal any feelings of rejection from your mother that touched that embryo. I ask that the Lord Jesus would bless and bathe that little embryo in His own precious blood and shield it from all harm.

There is complete safety only in Jesus' love. His love makes up for any deficiency in human love. With Jesus present there is only peace and security in love.

As your father discovers that he will be a father, I ask the Lord to bless the relationship of father and child. I ask that He shield this tender life from any fear, trepidation, or rejection. I ask that He heal any negativity that springs from society, relatives, or friends. I ask that the Lord would watch over that little fetus as it develops and grows within the womb of its mother, loving and protecting it at every moment.

The Lord Jesus is present on the day of your birth. As this child comes forth into the world, the Lord Jesus is there to hold, to embrace, to rejoice, and to give thanks. Now picture Jesus holding you as a newborn child. It is Jesus who presents you to your mother. The Lord blesses her motherhood.

If you are adopted, picture yourself being handed to your adoptive mother, as the Lord Jesus says, "Here, I have a gift for you."

Know that your mother wanted to be the best mother she could possibly be. Forgive her now for any mistakes she made, anything that was lacking in her motherhood.

Jesus takes you, infant child, from your mother and hands you to your father, adoptive father, or foster father. He says to him, "I have a gift." Your father looks down upon you. He loves you tremendously and is proud of everything that you are. In his heart he resolves to be the best father he can possibly be.

See yourself being held by your father as Jesus stands over you. He blesses that fatherhood. Forgive your father for all his mistakes and inadequacies.

Let the Lord bless all three — mother, father, and infant child. His hand is on you as He blesses you. You are His special child. His blessing will be with you at every moment in the future.

Lord, we give You thanks for Your protection and for Your love. We give You thanks for all Your blessings. Thank You, Lord, for Your love and Your presence.

14

HEALED BY LOVE

The LORD consoles His people.
He takes pity on the afflicted.
For they were saying,
 "The Lord has abandoned us.
The Lord has forgotten us."
Does a woman forget her baby at the breast?
Does she fail to cherish the son of her womb?
Yet even if these forget,
I will never forget you.
See, I have you branded on the palm
 of my hands....

The mountains may fall,
and the hills be shaken,
but My love for you will never cease.
My covenant of peace with you will never
 be shaken.

           Isaiah 49:13–16; 54:10

Throughout the Scriptures we read about God's faithful love for His people. We learn about His fatherly care and concern. The Lord constantly calls His people to trust Him and to surrender every burden to Him. God wants His children to have confidence that He does care for them. He will never abandon or forsake His people. That is His consistent promise.

Many people have a problem with trust. They have been hurt in some ways in their past and carry the burden of life's disappointments in their hearts. These experiences become a heaviness that deadens joy and banishes hope. It is difficult for such people to surrender in loving confidence to God's fatherly care. It is difficult for one who is bowed down under the weight of sorrow to look up and look ahead in life.

How can a person who has never had a human father's love understand and accept God's fatherly love? How can a person who knew child abuse or who had an alcoholic or absent parent now understand God's tender care? These are important issues.

The prophetic word from Isaiah at the beginning of this chapter offers healing. God's love is even deeper than the love of a mother or father. It is a faithful and dependable love that will supply the security that broken trust has stolen.

People carry two kinds of hurt. The obvious hurts occur when a person is betrayed, misunderstood, rejected, ridiculed, or slandered. These are hurts that can be readily recalled and even relived. In fact, oftentimes these experiences are difficult to forget. They leave memories of tangible pain that can hurt deeply for years.

Another kind of hurt is more subtle. This type does not lie in memories but rather in a lack of memories. It is not what happened but what did not happen that causes pain — a lack of love, an absence, or a void. A person needed someone for help, support, friendship, and understanding, and no one met those needs. Sometimes the person who should have understood did not understand. The one who should have been the emotional support was insensitive. The result is a feeling of abandonment and loneliness, a hollow ache in the heart.

The cause of the lack of memories can be as obvious as a missing, ill, alcoholic, or neglectful parent who never gave the care and tender affection that was needed by the child. It can also be the loss of someone else who was deeply loved. Grief, anger, and all the disappointment and confusion caused by a death can live on in a person for years.

A person might feel unfulfilled and restless and never entirely at home in any one place. Even when experiencing love, the love does not suffice. One cannot suddenly begin to trust when trust has been lacking for years, when trust has been betrayed, or if trust was never part of life. Such deep emptiness can cause a paralysis of the heart.

Yet God calls us to trust Him. God wants to meet our human needs with healing love. All those hollow aches can be healed. The emptiness can be filled; the void can be touched; the hunger can be satisfied. Faith speaks of a fullness of life and love that is found in Christ Jesus and given us by His Spirit. This is healing of the hurts of the heart and is very much a work of grace.

The human need for love is so great that only a great love can meet it adequately. Only divine love can fill the soul's empty places. Jesus imparts that great love to us.

Free to Love

I have seen many instances in which people have been healed by the faithful love of the Lord. One example would be that of a woman I'll call Sue, who had a fear of getting close to people. As a result she was isolated and lonely.

Many people who were very close to Sue had died. She was nine when her father died very suddenly. Two years later her brother died in a drowning accident. Later Sue's fiancé died in a tragic accident. Those accumulated hurts left in her a deep sense that it was dangerous to get close to people. It was dangerous to love anyone, because it seemed that the people she loved would die and abandon her. As much as Sue wanted and needed someone to love and share her life, she ended relationships and pushed people away.

In time Sue found faith and developed a relationship with Jesus Christ. She learned that it was safe to love Jesus, because He would never abandon her. People spent a lot of time praying for Sue. That healing prayer deepened her sense of the Lord's faithful love, which filled the place in her heart that had known only fear of loss. She was able to find friends and have relationships more freely than before.

Joe had never known his father's love. His father had an alcohol problem and thus was never present for him. Joe didn't receive the strong masculine love that he needed. He didn't know how to give and to share love. Intimacy was almost impossible for him.

With prayer and ministry, the healing love of the Father filled Joe's inner needs. He learned to call God "Abba," surrendered in trust to Him, and found security and inner peace. He learned that he could trust God as Father and friend, just as Jesus had done.

God's love is spiritual, but it is also very real. It can fill empty places in the human heart, feed the spiritual hunger of the soul, and calm the restless spirit with peace. When Jesus gives us His Spirit, it is a real and tangible gift of love that is more than capable of filling the heart and supplying what is lacking in human love.

Less obvious was the situation of Helen, who had a constant sense of anxiety that the people she loved and needed would one day not be there for her. She felt that people would abandon her, especially when she most needed them. The perplexing part was that she came from a stable home. She had loving parents and a secure family situation growing up.

One memory in particular surfaced while Helen was receiving prayer ministry. It was a simple incident in itself, but it was very traumatic for the small child she had been. She recalled a day when she had come home from school deeply distressed and in tears after being hurt by a classmate. It was not a big hurt, but she felt rejected and misunderstood.

Helen expected to find comfort in her mother's loving arms and a word of encouragement and understanding. She knew that her mother would listen and dry her tears. But her mother had gone out shopping. Helen was deeply disappointed.

For a little girl, small hurts can be easily magnified. Small instances can be felt deeply, and this one created profound anxiety and insecurity for Helen. Reason and logic fall short when a hurt is lodged in the human spirit, deeper than the rational mind can reach. Only the Holy Spirit can touch the human spirit with healing peace and comfort.

With prayer, counseling, and faith, Helen found that healing. Prayer touched her spirit, where the hurts were lodged, where they had festered and caused ongoing distress. Now Helen has found security in the Lord

The Way of Prayer

Two things are essential to healing the aches of the heart caused by a lack of affirming love. They are healing prayer and supportive ministry.

This healing prayer is not the kind of prayer that is said once and then answered overnight. Rather it is an ongoing process. The person prayerfully and spiritually goes back over the years and allows the healing love of the Lord to touch moments of emptiness and fill the voids in the heart. The person's inner self and the small child carried in the unconscious mind need to be bathed in the security of God's love and the warmth of His presence.

Of primary importance in the process is the need to forgive the person who was not there. Joe had to forgive his alcoholic father for being inadequate as a father. Helen had to forgive her mother for being absent at a time when she most needed her. People are not always responsible for what they did not do or could not do. But forgiveness is still necessary because of the effects left in the heart by the absences.

It is even essential to forgive loved ones who have died and thus left emptiness in the heart. It is important to extend that forgiveness to God, who allows people to die.

Once forgiveness is offered, healing prayer will allow the love of Jesus to go back in one's life, using the active imagination, touch the times of emptiness, loneliness, and loss, and then fill those voids with His love. We can say such a healing prayer for ourselves or for another person, always using a gentle voice and an affirming, positive tone. We can repeat it at different times for different periods in life and for different memories. This prayer is very powerful if the heart is open and disposed to receive healing grace.

For the healing of those who feel unloved, we pray

> *Lord, with Your love fill in all the empty places of the heart where love is lacking. Make up for any deficiency by Your loving presence, by Your loving Spirit. Make up the difference between the love that was needed in life, which was great, and the love that was received, which was much too small.*

Lord Jesus, allow the Spirit of Your love to flow deeply within the wounds and broken places of the spirit. Fill in all the empty places of the heart. Bring healing. Bring security. Bring Your affirming love.

Parents can say this prayer for their children as they realize their own deficiencies and failures in parenthood. (No one is perfect, and it is impossible to be a perfect parent.) Parents have a special role in praying for their children because of the natural spiritual bond that unites them. A parent can pray over the child while the child is sleeping, because it is a time of quiet rest and there are no distractions to receiving grace. The prayer can include the laying on of hands. It can be prayed as a prayer of intercession, even if the child is not present.

For the healing of a child, the parent prays

Lord, fill in the gaps. Fill in all the empty places of my child's heart with Your love. Make up the difference between the love that I was able to give and the love that my child so desperately needed.

Beyond Prayer

Besides praying for healing, it is also important to minister healing. A person who was never sufficiently affirmed in love or who has a hollow ache left by abandonment and disappointment needs to be secure in love in the here and now. We do not outgrow the need to be affirmed and understood, loved, and appreciated. Love is an essential need of every human being.

Generally speaking, loving affirmation is not found in society at large. Isolation, egoism, and self-reliance are more the norm in our world. Competition and rivalry are common. People pay large amounts of money to counselors who will listen to them and try to understand their inner pain. Granted, many people are wonderfully helped with counseling; thank God for that.

That being said, however, what is needed and what works more naturally are good friendships with caring, loving people who accept and affirm one another. A Christian whose life is rooted in the Gospel should expect to live within a framework of loving, supportive relationships called a *community*, with other Christians who have their lives rooted in that same Lord Jesus.

Relationships within a community are friendships. Anyone who ministers healing must also be a friend who cares, supports, and affirms the other. But the minister's affirmation needs to be complemented by the support of a loving community of some kind, a community of believers. It is both hurtful and frustrating to pray for people and then have them return to the same environment where they get bruised again and again.

We all need to be supported, to be loved, and to be secure in love. If affirmation and encouragement were lacking in one's early years, they should all the more be found in later years. We are all part of one another and have responsibility to others. The Lord tells us, "By this will all men know that *you* are *My* disciples; that *you* have love *for one another*" (John 13:35).

So we pray for good friendships and for the redemption of society, even as we pray for healing for the bruised and broken ones. We ask the Lord to raise up communities and families where people can be accepted and affirmed as unique individuals and invited and encouraged to become whole, secure, and fulfilled as God wills them to be.

For the healing that is needed now, we pray

Lord Jesus, by Your presence and through the Spirit of Your love at work within us, fill all the gaps and empty places between the love we need each day and the love we actually receive. We pray that by Your presence, love, and tender concern, we will know healing of the hurts and be brought to the fullness of Your love in peace and joy.

15

CONFRONTING THE EVIL ONE

Grow strong in the Lord. Put on the armor of God so you will be able to resist the devil's tactics. It is not against human enemies that we have to struggle, but against the sovereignties and the powers that originate in darkness. We struggle against a spiritual army of evil in the heavens. This is why you must rely on God's armor, or you will not be able to put up any resistance when the worst happens. If you do not rely upon the power of God, you will not have enough resources to hold your ground.

Ephesians 6:10–13

This challenging text has been the subject of study and discussion for centuries, and much has been written on it by way of commentary. It confronts us with a stark reality of the spiritual life: a world of evil, a satanic kingdom, demonic activity, and spiritual warfare.

Because of fear and ignorance surrounding this teaching, more often than not it is downplayed and even ridiculed as superstition. Ignoring the issue of a demonic reality is definitely easier than confronting it. But when people delve into the spiritual realm, seek to understand something of the mystery of evil, and touch on the deep spiritual struggles of people, the truth of what St. Paul wrote becomes more obvious. The human struggle is not always against flesh and blood but often against sovereignties, principalities, and other spiritual powers.

In theological and philosophical terms, evil is a deficiency: It is a lack of goodness and harmony, a disruption in God's order. But evil can also be understood as an active personal force. However shadowy and obscure it seems to be, evil is at work in the world, bringing serious consequences for people.

Discerning the Darkness

Experience teaches that sickness has three basic origins. Healing ministers will find themselves praying differently depending on the cause of the illness.

The first source of sickness, the most obvious one, is physical in nature. Something is not working right in the body — maybe there is a chemical imbalance or a biological breakdown. Something real and identifiable is working against the body, such as a virus or bacterium. The healing minister must ask the Lord to restore balance, repair damage, heal infection, and bring physical strength to the person.

The second category of illness is psychosomatic illness. This kind of illness originates within one's inner self — within the mind and the spirit of the person. The disease is very real but is somehow intertwined and interlocked with the person's subconscious and conscious mind. The healing minister needs to pray for underlying problems as well as the obvious physical ailment. This requires discernment and sensitivity to the issues people deal with that run deeper than the obvious physical ailment.

A third category of illness is the demonic, or the diabolical. We need to be well aware of the reality and danger of the black arts, witchcraft, Satan worship, and other such occult practices, with their curses, spells, and hexes of various degrees of seriousness and effectiveness. These are not playful games for active imaginations.

In November of 1972, Pope Paul VI gave a talk that surprised many people. He asked, "What is one of the greatest needs of the Church today?" His response was the need for the Church to acknowledge the reality of the Satanic realm. He asserted that Satan is a real individual, a personal spiritual being who exerts great influence in the world and even in the Church.

The pope's talk was greeted with much skepticism and ridicule at the time. It was called a superstitious throwback to more primitive days. Critics said that he was playing on people's fears using medieval fantasies and outdated nonsense. Many learned and educated theologians and scholars publicly denied that there was any reality to the demonic realm.

However, anyone with experience in the ministry of healing recognizes the truth of what Pope Paul VI was saying. He was, in fact, speaking a prophetic word. Many people in our day are caught up in and deeply wounded by demonic realities. In addition to black magic and other forms of the occult, demons are at work in more subtle ways to block the work of God. This is a reality that we ignore at our own risk

Fascination, Fear, and the Fight

Society has a very complex and somewhat contradictory relationship to the demonic dimension of reality. On one hand is the denial and ridicule to which I've already alluded, and on the other hand is fear and fascination. Pointing to this fascination is the box-office popularity of such movies as *The Exorcist* and *The Rite*. Books about demonic possession, the Antichrist, the occult, and witchcraft are best-sellers. Shows about haunted places, unexplained spiritual phenomena, and various experiences of spirits and ghosts are common on television. Experimentation with the occult — through games, for instance — is particularly attractive to young people. There can be serious consequences to this kind of activity.

I recall some female college students who came to church in a terrible state of agitation. They had been playing an occult game, and one girl had offered herself as a bride to Satan. Then something had happened.

The room had become ice cold, and "there was something there." The previously hopeful bride was seized with ungodly terror and anguish. The other girls were terrified.

The adults in charge at the college wrote the experience off as superstition and overactive imaginations. But the girls knew better. They had strayed into an area that they did not understand and could not control. They could not shake a dark and fearful presence. So they came to the church for help.

The prayer was not complicated, but it was intense. The girls had to repent and take back anything they had given to Satan. The would-be bride had to consciously renounce her offer. Everything needed to be done in the name of Jesus.

We invoked the power and the Spirit of Jesus, and we blessed the girls in His precious name. We called upon the blood of Jesus, which had made them Christians and cleansed them of sin, as the assurance of God's claim on them, a claim more powerful than the claim of darkness. Finally, every girl renewed her baptismal promises, her renunciation of Satan, and her faith in Jesus Christ.

Some people see evil at work everywhere and are overcome by fear. Some believe that all manner of problems, illnesses, and sufferings are caused by the direct intervention of Satan. They see demons everywhere. This fascination ends by glorifying what should never be glorified — the satanic world.

Over the centuries the Church's teachings have maintained a good balance regarding the work of evil and the occult. Basing herself on the Scriptures, the Church teaches that Satan does exist but that his kingdom of darkness has been defeated by Jesus Christ. St. John tells us that the whole world is in the hands of the evil one. But he also says that by His cross and resurrection, the Lord Jesus has freed the world from the dominion of Satan (see 1 John 4:3–5, 9–10; 5:5).

This is not a contest between two equal powers. Christians are not mere pawns in a spiritual battle between the forces of good and evil. Rather, the baptized Christian shares in the victory of Christ. By His cross Jesus has defeated Satan. By His resurrection He has gained victory for everyone.

There is reason to have a healthy respect for the demonic world, but there is no reason to fear. Hell trembles at the very name of Jesus.

Scripture says to resist Satan and stand firm against his kingdom, his work, and his deceits. "Hold fast and stand your ground" is the admonition of St Paul (see Ephesians 6:14; Philippians 4:1; 1 Thessalonians 3:8). He tells us to take up sword and shield and to put on a helmet and a breastplate, that our "feet should be shod with the readiness of the Gospel" (Ephesians 6:15).

St. Paul is speaking about a kind of warfare. Soldiers wore footgear so they could dig in, not be pushed back. They would be able to stand firm against the enemy. Our footgear is the Gospel, which is a grounding of faith in the Resurrection and in the victory of Jesus. We are not to run, cower, or hide before evil but to stand fast, look it squarely in the eye without fear, and claim victory over it.

Satan, or the power of evil, can be said to be very much like a chained dog who barks menacingly. A chained dog can do only one thing — frighten people. He can cause no harm unless someone comes too close. One neither plays games with the occult nor trembles before it.

Victory Is Ours

Scripture makes it very clear that Jesus had a twofold ministry: to preach and to heal. He accomplished the latter sometimes by touch, sometimes by command, sometimes by casting out a demon. We read that Jesus cast out a demon that was mute, or in other words, was causing the victim to be mute. When the demon left, the man could speak (Matthew 9:32–33; Luke 11:14). Other stories show a connection between casting out a demon and healing (see Matthew 12:22, for example).

Jesus shared His ministry with the disciples, commissioning them to continue His work. He equipped them for this by imparting His Spirit to them, the very Spirit at work in Him. He sent them out to preach the Kingdom with that power, and He added a twofold commission: to heal the sick and to cast out demons (see Matthew 10:1; Mark 3:14).

The disciples went out, preaching and healing. Scripture tells us that when they returned to the Lord, "they were simply overjoyed that the demons submitted to them when they used the name of Jesus" (Luke 10:17). Jesus shares that same authority with His whole Church, imparting the Holy

Spirit so that His work will continue through time. "Those on whom you lay your hands will recover, and demons will submit to you when you use My name" (Mark 16:17–18).

Sometimes it is necessary in the healing ministry, or even in daily life, to stand firm against the powers of evil and break their grip on people. We do not come across this too often, but it does happen.

When I was a young, newly ordained priest, I had a memorable and striking experience while visiting a man in the hospital. The man was a member of the parish, and I had come for a pastoral visit and to pray with him. While visiting I learned of a patient in the next room named Charles. This man had been in the hospital for several weeks.

Charles had symptoms such as low-grade fever, generalized aches and pains, swelling, and stiffness. His blood tests showed there was a problem, and yet they pointed to nothing specific. The medical professionals conducted a lot of tests, followed by even more testing. Every test showed something but nothing specific or definitive.

Charles was suffering terribly. He had a great deal of pain. He experienced sleepless nights, and almost every evening he had night terrors. These created deep anxiety and fears.

I prayed with Charles, and I did something that I had never done before, something spontaneous and unexpected on my part: I broke a curse in the name of Jesus. As I did, Charles's whole body reacted by arching in the bed. Tears began flowing from his eyes.

I continued praying, and I continued to break any curse that could have been placed on Charles from any source. As an afterthought, I replaced every curse with a blessing, simply because it seemed a logical thing to do. Eventually his body relaxed. He fell into a deep sleep.

In due time Charles's blood counts returned to normal, his fever disappeared, and the aches vanished. Within four days he was ready to go home. There never was an adequate diagnosis of his sickness, nor was it ever explained how or why he recovered. It was considered one of those medical mysteries that happen. But I knew in my heart that Charles had somehow been cursed and that the curse had been broken.

I also knew that there was a lesson to be learned, and so I pondered and thought about the experience many times. Everyone in our hospitals does not suffer from curses. It is possible, however, that some do. Christians should be very conscious and aware of the authority that they received with baptism. We should also be aware of the satanic reality that we face and of the fact that as Christians, we have both authority and victory over it.

The Power of Jesus' Blood

A traditional and time-tested way to pray against evil or suspected demonic activity is to claim the power of the blood of Jesus. In the Pentecostal churches, claiming the "power of the blood of Jesus" is almost a catch phrase. Songs such as "There Is Power in the Blood" are constantly sung. The blood of Jesus *is* indeed a great weapon against the forces of evil, and a prayer that claims that power will be very effective.

It is not only the Pentecostal and fundamentalist Christians who have a devotion to the blood of Jesus. There is a long-standing practice of prayer to the Precious Blood of Jesus in the Catholic tradition as well. Congregations of priests and nuns proudly bear the name of the Precious Blood. Novenas, litanies, and other prayers attest to the devotional celebration of the blood of Jesus in the Church's tradition.

The blood of Jesus is powerful against the demonic for three reasons. The first is that the blood of Jesus is the price of our salvation.

All humans are born into a state of original sin, the result of Adam's sin. By our very birth we are stained by unredeemed darkness. Salvation means redemption out of this unfortunate state. Jesus came to redeem the children of Adam by His death on the cross. His blood is our ransom. His blood has brought us out of darkness and into light. His blood is poured out in love as the gift and grace of salvation. To claim the blood of Jesus is to claim one's identity as redeemed in Christ.

Secondly, the blood of Jesus was shed for the forgiveness of sin, the one barrier that stands between each person and God. Scripture tells us that there is no forgiveness of sin without the shedding of blood (Hebrews 9:22). The blood of Jesus brings that forgiveness, overcoming the barrier between God and His people.

Thirdly, the blood of Jesus is the blood of the new covenant (Matthew 26:28). His blood unites us to the Father. The covenant "in His blood" is the unity of hearts and souls in the love that was originally meant to be.

So the blood of Jesus — the price of our salvation, shed for the forgiveness of sin, the blood of the new covenant — is exactly what has destroyed Satan's kingdom and his claim on humanity. Therefore, praying by the power of the blood of Jesus is a very strong prayer to use against evil and any suspected satanic activity.

We belong to God, not to the darkness. By Jesus' death and the blood He shed on the cross, we are ransomed from the kingdom of evil and brought into the Kingdom of God. We are forgiven and pardoned of sin.

Evil has no claim on someone who is redeemed and for-given and cleansed by the blood of Jesus. Satan has no power or authority. Only God and His Kingdom have the ultimate claim on someone who has been purchased, ransomed, and redeemed by the blood of Jesus.

And so we pray

Lord Jesus, we pray in the power of Your precious blood, shed for our sins and for our redemption. Because of Your blood, shed out of love, all our sins are forgiven, and the punishment for sin is cancelled. Shield us from all danger and harm and the punishment that sin would bring upon us. Protect us from evil.

By Your most precious blood, Jesus, break all bond-age to the evil one. Let the power of Your blood bring healing to our lives, to our minds, and to our bodies. Cover us and cleanse us with Your blood. Heal us by the power of Your most precious blood, Lord Jesus.

Thank You for the gift of Your love and the forgive-ness of sin proven by the shedding of Your blood. Without grace we are all lost. With Your grace we are redeemed and restored to friendship with You.

Satan has no claim on us and no hold on us. We belong to You and Your Kingdom. In You is our safety, peace, and security. In You we find life and healing, for-giveness, and peace, because You shed Your blood and gave Your life for our redemption. Thank You for such great love and mercy.

16

THE MYSTERY OF SUFFERING

It makes me happy to suffer for you, and I
am suffering now. I rejoice in my sufferings
because I make up in my own body what is
still to be undergone by Christ for the sake
of His body, the Church.

Colossians 1:24

In this most unusual statement, St. Paul claims that he is actually happy to suffer. The fact is that most people find anguish, not joy, in suffering.

Everyone has to grapple with suffering in some way, because life presents myriad experiences of pain and sorrow. Some people avoid suffering until it presses in on their reality. Others compile unanswered questions regarding the innocent who suffer and the good people who are not healed. People over the ages have brought many ideas and theories to the perplexing problem.

A minister of healing constantly confronts the deep mystery of suffering. It is important to think of it in light of the insights afforded by the Gospel. Faith brings a unique perspective.

Most importantly, God does not directly will suffering. The Gospel tells us He is a loving Father whose will is life and happiness, not misery and death. Jesus certainly demonstrated in His teaching and ministry that He did not will the suffering of anyone, whether it was of a physical, spiritual, or emotional nature. He healed sickness wherever He found it, affirming health and wholeness. This conviction underlies the entire healing ministry.

When sickness is healed, there is rejoicing. It is exciting to see the power of God at work, alleviating pain and anguish. But it highlights the problem that not everyone is healed. Even as faith-filled prayer for healing imitates the ministry of Jesus, people suffer. Why does God act in some cases and not in others?

Look to Jesus

Central to the mystery of suffering is the cross of Jesus Christ. The fact is that Jesus Himself, Beloved Son of God, suffered. The suffering He endured was not because He was being punished; He was "a man like us in all things but sin" (Eucharistic Prayer IV). He was perfect and loved by the Father.

Jesus embraced suffering because it is the lot of the human race that He came to save. By suffering He became one with the whole human family. He did not exempt Himself from life's challenges or its pain.

The suffering of Jesus, however, is redemptive, giving it a profound measure of value and good. His love for humanity brought Jesus to embrace the cross. By His suffering sins are forgiven, Satan is defeated, and our relationship with God is healed. All salvation is in the cross of Jesus.

It is not so much the agony Christ suffered that brings redemption. Many people suffer, and it is not considered salvation but rather tragedy and disaster. It is what Jesus brought to the cross that makes the difference.

Let's imagine a scenario quite different from what we know actually happened. Suppose Christ did not want to suffer. What if He turned His back on it, tried to run from it, but was taken against His will? One can imagine Christ being seized, tried, scourged, then dragged up the hill of Calvary, nailed to the cross, and left hanging there until He died.

In this fantasy many facts would remain the same. Christ would have suffered exactly as He did. He would have been crowned with thorns. He would have been crucified. He would have shed His blood. But the world would not have found salvation in His suffering. His death would have been just as tragic and painful, just as bloody and unjust, but it would not have brought the forgiveness of sin.

What is redemptive about the cross of Jesus is the fact that He embraced it out of love for the Father and in humble obedience to the Father's will. He did it out of love for us. In the final analysis, it is love, not just the suffering, that redeems.

Daniel was a student I taught some years ago. We stayed in touch as he continued his education and began a career. One day he came to me to talk through a problem that he was having.

Daniel wanted to be married, but he did not want any children. Children, he thought, brought too many problems. They are expensive and demand a lot of time and attention. He could not imagine himself staying up all night with a crying baby or changing a diaper.

Eventually Daniel did get married, still with trepidation about children. As life unfolded, Daniel and his wife had a baby. Despite all the anxiety and fear, the child brought him great joy and happiness. In a way this was totally unexpected, which made it the more interesting.

Daniel loved his little girl with a passion that surprised him. He was totally taken by the helpless child who depended on him. He did the sleepless nights, the diaper changes, and all the things that parents do. He didn't seem to notice that these were the things he had feared. He enjoyed doing them and found more meaning in them than he could have imagined.

What changed? Love. Daniel was not engaging in chores, duties, drudgery, or obligation. He was acting out of love. Love transforms everything, even diaper changing.

More important than the fact that people suffer is the attitude with which they suffer. Many people are confined to a wheelchair and are in physical pain yet are actually filled with a joyful spirit. They have a sense of humor and a spark of vitality. Some sick and dying people give others more than they receive, because they can still love with a joyful and grateful heart. On the other hand, we all know people who are physically fit and healthy yet locked in prisons of anger, self-pity, and resentment.

Who is really degraded by suffering? The physically incapacitated person who has a heart and spirit that rise above physical limitations and circumstances, or the person who lives in a self-made prison of personal misery?

Suffering in and of itself does not ennoble a person. Suffering is a sad fact of reality that no one chooses. It can degrade people under crushing burdens. Yet suffering does not necessarily have the last word. Because the mind and will are free, a person can decide how to respond to the circumstances of life. It is possible to be ennobled by what one suffers with the proper attitude of the heart.

No one needs to be a captive to suffering or be controlled by it. That is the heart of the matter. Here is the lesson of the cross. Suffering did not conquer Jesus; He conquered suffering by love.

Kinds of Suffering

It is possible to distinguish three different kinds of suffering. The first is a kind of suffering that the Lord told us to be happy about. This is suffering visited upon us because of ministry or upholding Gospel values. There will be opposition as people are challenged by the Gospel and even offended by it, feeling judged and found wanting. This kind of suffering is a blessing, as Jesus told us: "Blessed are you when men persecute you, ridicule and laugh at you because of Me. Know then that your name is written in the Kingdom of Heaven" (Matthew 5:11–12). Jesus came not to bring peace but the sword (Matthew 10:34).

When St. Paul wrote that he rejoiced in his sufferings, he was saying that his ministry was faithful to the Gospel. He measured his success partially by the problems that his ministry caused. St. Paul was tired. He was misunderstood. He was persecuted. He was confronted by divisiveness and by people who ridiculed and opposed him. St. Paul found reason to rejoice in that fact, as though it were a confirmation that he was indeed working for the Lord.

Anyone who works authentically for Jesus can expect to encounter similar problems. In fact, if that does not happen, consider it good reason to question the authenticity of the ministry. As Jesus said, "Beware when they all speak well of you" (Luke 6:26).

Another kind of suffering comes not from the outside but from within the person as interior anguish and pain. This suffering arises from the whole array of fears, anxieties, doubts, mental anguish, grief, and sorrow that torments people. It comes from within the soul of the person, so to speak. The heart is broken, and the spirit is crushed. Many people carry these crosses in hidden sorrow and unseen pain. Others exhibit symptoms of depression and melancholy because of what they carry within. This is real suffering and requires healing.

A third kind of suffering is physical pain, the most obvious and common affliction of humanity. Many things divide the human race, but physical pain unites everyone in a common experience of suffering. This suffering can dominate one's life.

God does not directly will these last two types of suffering, the interior anguish and the physical suffering. These are not in and of themselves part of God's kingdom. Only by God's permissive will do they exist at all.

Suffering is in the world because evil is in the world. God's plan and purpose, revealed in Jesus, is to redeem the world from evil and consequently to alleviate suffering. If there is no immediate healing, it is at least possible for the suffering to be redeemed.

Sin and Suffering

It is critical to understand that no direct, personal correlation exists between sin and suffering. It is not valid to claim that people suffer as a consequence of their sins. God is not so petty that He would make someone sick to defend His wounded pride. Jesus demonstrates quite the opposite. He loves sinners and wants redemption and life for them, not punishment and suffering. He did not heal only good people; He came to sinners who would be thought to merit punishment and chastisement. God takes no delight in the suffering of anyone, saint or sinner.

Yet there is a correlation between sin and suffering: Because there is sin in the world, there is suffering in the world. It is a universal truth and not a personal vindictiveness of

God that links sin and suffering. Because of evil, something is awry in the world. Suffering results from the disorder.

The innocent suffer because they live in an evil world. The sun shines on the just and the unjust. Rain falls on the innocent and the guilty, Jesus told us (see Matthew 5:45). These are mysteries — the mystery of innocent suffering, the mystery of God's permissive will in allowing suffering, the mystery of why some escape suffering while others do not. The cross too is a mystery too deep for words. We can understand it in the spirit more than in the intellect.

The traditional way to respond to suffering is to "offer it up." There is truth in that advice, but it must be understood properly lest it become a trite phrase with more piety than meaning.

Suffering in and of itself is not from God, but like all things, it can be redeemed by the cross of Jesus Christ. The love of God shining in Jesus touches everything in human experience. Suffering is transformed to a new realm in the Spirit, redeemed and even, one could say, sanctified and potentially sanctifying.

In chapter 5 of Ephesians, St. Paul wrote, "You were once in darkness, but now you are light in the Lord. Anything that is exposed by the light will be illuminated. What is illuminated turns into light" (Ephesians 5:8–9). Now, suffering is something dark and destructive in itself. Useless suffering can crush the heart and the soul. But when it is transformed, brought into the Kingdom of God and redeemed by the cross of Jesus, something destructive becomes sanctifying.

The Gospels tell us that while Christ was on the cross, it was the hour of darkness (see Matthew 27:45; Mark 15:33; Luke 23:44). Yet Christ used this horrific experience to redeem the world. The hour of darkness became a great light, in a sense. It became the vehicle of salvation. Love shone in and through that darkness that became redemption for all.

People who suffer in any way are able to "offer it up" — that is, to unite their sufferings to the cross of Jesus. By so doing they can transform their sufferings into a work of salvation. It can be helpful to offer up suffering for a very specific purpose, such as for vocations, the conversion of a sinner, or the healing of a relationship.

I knew a woman who was dying of cancer and who was in a great deal of pain. Sonya was a person of deep faith who had a personal relationship to Jesus. The misfortune of her life was that her husband had been abusive and unfaithful, and he did not share her faith. But Sonya loved her husband and desired to see him saved. She consciously offered her suffering in union with Jesus for his salvation.

Several things were revealed by this act of sacrifice. It was obvious that Sonya's love for her husband was authentic. She truly desired that he be blessed and forgiven. Her love knew mercy. Because of this she suffered with a great deal of peace and tranquility, almost joyfully, as she became an instrument in the hands of God.

Before Sonya died, her husband asked her forgiveness for his failures and sins against her. He went to confession and was reconciled to God. He had a true conversion experience. Sonya died in great peace, and her husband was a man transformed.

To heal suffering would seem to be the first desire of every heart. But to redeem suffering is also part of God's plan. St. Paul rejoices in his sufferings because he is united to Jesus in the work of salvation. Calvary is where Jesus unites Himself to all suffering humanity and where suffering humanity is united to Jesus.

And so we pray

We take each suffering, pain, and heartache, all that we are carrying within, and we unite it to the Lord Jesus Christ as He suffers upon the cross. We offer all to the glory of the Father, in loving obedience to His will, with all its mystery. We pray that the suffering we offer may be for the good of the world, the salvation of sinners, the sanctification of the Church, and [name a specific intention].

St. Paul tells us to give thanks for all things. So for the sorrows of life and the pains we carry too we give thanks, in humble obedience and in union with the Savior. Amen.

17

THE PRAYER OF FAITH

If someone is in trouble, he should pray. If
someone is feeling happy, he should sing a
psalm. If one of you is ill, he should send for
the elders of the Church. They must anoint
him with oil in the name of the Lord Jesus
and pray over him. The prayer of faith will
save the one who is sick, and the Lord will
raise him up again.

James 5:13–15

The heart of the matter is in the final sentence of this quote
from James: the prayer of faith will save the one who is sick.
The practical directions that St. James gives support that
prayer of faith — calling in the elders, anointing with oil, and
ministering to the sick person. The essential thing is to pray
for the healing with faith.

On one level this text can be understood as a reference
to the Anointing of the Sick that is one of the seven sacraments. A sacrament is a privileged and unique working of
grace in the Church, normally at the hands of a priestly minister, which the believing community reverence with faith
and celebrate with devotion. A sacrament "works" because
the Lord Jesus is at work in His Church. The priest ministers
in the name of the Lord Jesus.

Beyond that, the sacrament should be faith-filled in order to be experienced most richly and effectively. The priest prays for healing as a continuation of the ministry of Jesus. The sick person and the minister should expect the Lord to honor the prayer of the Church. It is the prayer of Jesus Himself together with the whole Church.

I often anoint the sick after Mass, because I believe that the greatest healing comes through the Eucharist. During the Mass I encourage people to enter into the healing process by taking their needs and infirmities to the Lord at the very moment they receive the Eucharist. After the liturgy the Holy Eucharist is exposed on the altar for adoration as people come forward for healing prayer. With the Holy Eucharist within and exposed before all, we are embraced by the merciful heart of Jesus.

When a layman prays for healing, it is not a sacrament but a sacramental. While the sacrament has an effectiveness all its own, made more fruitful by faith, the sacramental needs faith to render it effective.

From the Heart

The prayer of faith is a prayer filled with trust, hope, and confidence. It is more than a vague hope that someone in heaven might hear the prayer. Rather it expresses a real and active faith in the loving presence of Jesus to His people. It is a faith that is based on the promises of Scripture. Words do not bring healing; Jesus brings healing in the power of the Spirit in response to a prayer from the heart of a faithful person.

Some people are comfortable with formal prayers that can be recited by memory or read from a book. When accompanied by confidence in the Lord, this type of prayer can be effective. Yet a formal prayer is not always the same thing as a prayer of faith.

A prayer of faith comes from a full heart. It is not read but spoken in personal words from the inner depths of a person. There must be a real and living faith at work to ground the prayer and render it effective. Jesus Himself warned against thinking that a sheer multiplication of words will win a hearing in God's presence. It is not words but faith that counts.

Recently I received an e-mail from a woman who had cancer. Deborah had read a testimonial on the Internet from a woman who went to a healing Mass, "received healing prayer," and was cured of cancer. Deborah asked that I send her a copy of the prayer that was used.

I tried to explain that the healed woman was referring not to a written prayer or a formula but to a heartfelt prayer of faith. Our poor Deborah could not conceive of spontaneous prayer from the heart. She insisted that there had to be something that she could read or recite. In the end I sent Deborah a prayer, very similar to the one that closes this chapter. She was satisfied with that, as I am sure the Lord was. And her request gave me a deeper appreciation of the situation in the Church today.

It is more important to stand before God and speak from the heart than to recite pious phrases that lack true feeling. An authentic and heartfelt prayer for healing can be these words said honestly: "Lord, I don't quite believe, but I believe enough to be here. I believe enough to reach out to You. I ask You with a faith that is riddled with doubt to please touch my sick friend [my wife, my husband] and bring healing." That is a real prayer from the heart and truly expresses what is within the person.

A prayer may even be tinged with anger. Moses prayed before the Lord with some anger (see Exodus 33:12). An honest prayer for healing is the prayer of faith of which St. James writes. It comes from the heart and is sincere and real.

The Role of Faith

The Gospels speak of the necessity of faith for healing. Jesus said a number of times, "Your faith has made you well" (Mark 5:34; Luke 8:48; 17:19; 18:42). Another time He said, "Let it be done to you in accordance with your faith, or in proportion to your faith" (Matthew 9:29). St. Paul once met a crippled person and saw that he "had the faith to be healed" (Acts 14:8–10). Usually the one who is sick and is receiving prayer needs to have some degree of faith in order to be open to what God is doing.

However, we need to avoid extremes. Some people exaggerate the role of faith in the healing process, making it the most important and an absolutely necessary factor for healing. The minister might read a Scripture passage, chapter and verse, reminding God and the sick person of all the promises that God has made. The one who is sick often responds with tremendous effort to work up and affirm his or her faith.

In this light it seems that if a healing does not take place, the person must lack sufficient faith. It is as though there is a definite, almost mathematical proportion between the degree of faith the person has and the healing that will take place. Hesitancy and doubts are understood as major blocks to healing.

There is some truth here. We need to have faith, and faith needs to be rooted in the promises of Scripture. If the role of faith is exaggerated, however, there is a risk of Pelagianism, the oldest heresy of all. Pelagianism taught that a person is saved by personal effort rather than a savior. In other words, grace is not a necessity but only an aid to salvation. Piety, prayer, the practice of virtue, and good works are understood to be the essential means of salvation and healing.

But no one is saved by works, no matter what the work. Everything is grace or gift. Faith neither saves nor heals; Jesus does.

When faith is emphasized as essential to healing, we risk leaving the sick person in a state of guilt and confusion if a healing does not take place. The person may feel that lack of faith is responsible for the lack of healing. He or she needs to try harder to have more faith, better faith, or a purer faith so that healing can occur. Something of God's love is lost and replaced by a burden of responsibility that can be oppressive and anything but healing.

Yes, faith is necessary and essential. But it is not a legalistic faith. Rather it is faith that is trust. Anyone who goes to the Lord for healing approaches with faith and with trust — trust in His love, His compassion, His wisdom, His mercy, and His power. Contrary to the tension created by trying to have a faith of the right kind is this release of the entire burden to the Lord in total confidence and surrender. That is the kind of faith for which the Lord asks. It is total trust.

The Lord teaches that faith the size of a mustard seed, the smallest of all seeds, can move mountains (see Matthew 17:20). He is not talking so much about the amount of faith as about the kind of faith. Faith the size of a mustard seed is enough to enter into the presence of God and say, "Lord, I believe. Help my unbelief" (Mark 9:24).

Simple Prayer

This faith is also what the Lord was referring to when He said that we should be like children. We need to have childlike confidence in the fact that God is Father; He can be called "Abba" or "Daddy." He does care for His children. All confident prayer relies on that basic fact. Just as a person speaks to his own father with words that come from the heart rather than words that are written down or memorized, a childlike prayer is spontaneous as well as simple and real. The language of prayer does not need to be holy or pious; it needs to be real.

I will always remember one parish mission that included a healing service. I was a very young priest at the time, and all this was still new to me and to most of the Church actually. It was exciting and bold to be praying for healing in a parish church. All the people who had physical, spiritual, mental, or emotional needs were invited to come up to the priest and ask for prayer. The priest laid hands upon each one and asked the Lord for a blessing and a healing — it was that simple.

An altar boy of about eleven stood beside me as I prayed over people. Jake held the vial with oil for anointing. After I had prayed for a few people, I asked Jake if he would like to join me in praying because he showed a keen interest in and a sense of compassion for the sick and hurting people. As he held the vial of oil in one hand, Jake reached out and placed his other hand on the shoulder of the person who came forward. He did it very naturally, very spontaneously, and with beautiful, childlike simplicity and confidence.

After we had prayed over a few more people, I asked Jake if he would like to say a prayer as he placed his hand on the person. So following my blessing and anointing with oil, that young altar boy would make up his own spontaneous prayer from his heart, asking the Father to heal and to bless the person. Many people were touched, and I am sure that many of Jake's prayers were answered.

A prayer of faith comes from the heart, not a book. No one needs special training, refined theology, education, or degrees to pray for healing.

Speaking out a prayer builds faith — for the one who prays it and for the ones who hear it. Verbalizing is important so that those praying together can agree on what is being prayed for. The Gospels say that where two or three agree on anything, it will be a powerful prayer before the throne of grace (see Matthew 18:20). Everyone can hear the petition and say *Amen*, and with that the prayer becomes a united prayer.

As I mentioned before, this is not always as simple as it would first seem. In fact, people sometimes pray in different ways for different things, even when there appears to be a single purpose to the ministry. Some might be praying for a miracle, some for wisdom for the medical staff, and some for a happy and peaceful death. It is important that there be agreement in the prayer, so that the *Amen* is authentic and meaningful.

Many factors will come into play in a prayer for healing, depending on the circumstances and the actual sickness being prayed for. For example, if there is a germ or virus, we ask the Lord to cast it out. If there is a growth, such as a cancer or a tumor, we ask the Lord to make His healing rays of light fall upon it and shrink it or burn it out. Where parts of the body have died, such as nerve endings or cells, we pray to the Holy Spirit, the Giver of Life, to restore and renew what has been damaged.

It is important for people who pray for healing to expect the Spirit of God to lead the prayer. God dwells within every baptized person. St. Paul says that when we do not know how to pray, the Spirit comes to help us. He intercedes with words that are not our own (see Romans 8:26–27). If anyone feels uncomfortable praying spontaneously, it is helpful to ask the Spirit of God to lead the prayer.

Praying for the sick and ministering healing should not be awkward or forced. It should be comfortable, simple, personal, and authentic. A special physical stance is not necessary; the minister can stand beside the person or sit on the edge of the person's bed, perhaps with one hand placed gently on the shoulder or the head. Or one might simply hold the person's hand, a very human, comforting gesture.

What follows is a prayer for healing. The average prayer for healing is generally not as long as this one. Included are many different elements that could be put into a prayer. As much as you can, allow the Spirit to lead the prayer.

And so we pray

Father in heaven, I come before You in the name of Jesus Christ, who is Your Son and our Brother. I come before You strengthened through the intercession of Mary, whom Jesus has given to us as our mother. I come before You, Father, with thanksgiving and gratitude that I can approach You at all. I have free access before You, our God, who is our Father and the Creator of the whole universe. You are all-powerful. I thank You, Father, that Jesus has taught us to call You Abba, to call You Father, and that we have no fear in Your presence. Father, I thank You that I can be at home before You and speak from my heart to Your heart with confidence.

I pray now, Father, with great trust, knowing that You love and care about Your children and that You are concerned for each one personally. I thank You, Father, for Your great love and am inspired with confidence as I pray to You.

Father, the one that we both love is sick. The one that we both love is suffering. This sickness touches me deeply, because I care and therefore share the suffering and pain through love and compassion. Suffering with this loved one brings me to this prayer.

I know, Lord, if this means so much to me, how much more it must mean to You. You care for each of Your children. You sent your Son to die for us all. You love even more than I do.

Father, I stand before You as an unworthy sinner but also as Your child, in the name of Jesus, my brother and Your Son. I offer You the only perfect thing I have to offer — the wounds and the blood of Jesus. I offer You, Father, the perfect sacrifice of Your Son Jesus, and in the power of His Precious Blood I now pray.

I cover this person with the blood of Jesus and pray that all the healing power that is in the blood of Jesus might flow onto and through this person, touching the very places where Your touch is most needed. Touch the heart and the deep inner spirit. Fill in every void and touch every hollow, aching place. Let Your love bathe, fill, and flow through every physical and emotional space.

Send Your Spirit and the healing power of Your love to touch this physical ailment. Let Your healing power flow through to every broken, wounded, infected, diseased, and hurting place within. It is the power of Your love and compassion alone that heals.

Father, if there is an infection, cast it out and bring health and life. If there is any malignant growth, let Your light shine upon it, and let healing rays of love burn it out.

I pray that the Spirit, the Giver of Life, may move in power to revive and restore, renew and strengthen that which needs His touch. As Your love flows, bring health and new life to every cell, to every nerve ending, to every organ, and to every bodily system, and let Your peace come to restore hope and confidence and trust to the heart. Father, You are the Lord, and we are Your people, redeemed by the blood of Jesus and the sacrifice of the cross. Everything is now entrusted to You and to Your fatherly care.

Father, I can trust You because Jesus has taught me to trust You. Let this sickness be for Your glory. Allow us to see Your love powerfully at work as we see our loved one recover and regain strength, health, and new life. Fill us with joy, Lord, as we see You work.

Father, in the name of Jesus, I pray with gratitude and appreciation for Your deep and personal love. I pray with thanksgiving because I know that You hear and answer the prayer of faith. I trust in Your love. I trust in Your wisdom. I trust in Your goodness. I give You thanks now and always. Amen.

* ~